Router
Tips & Techniques

Router
Tips &
Techniques

BOB WEARING

2001

GUILD OF MASTER CRAFTSMAN PUBLICATIONS

First published 2001 by
Guild of Master Craftsman Publications Ltd,
166 High Street, Lewes,
East Sussex, BN7 1XN

Text, photographs and line illustrations © Bob Wearing 2001
Copyright in the Work © Guild of Master Craftsman Publications Ltd
Reprinted 2002

ISBN 1 86108 214 2

A catalogue record of this book is available from the British Library.

Black and white line illustrations by Bob Wearing
Colour illustrations by Simon Rodway from original line drawings by Bob Wearing
All photography by Bob Wearing with the exception of photographs of the author,
pages 2, 3, 4 (bottom) and 6 by Tim Roberts

Colour origination by Viscan Graphics (Singapore)

Printed and bound by Kyodo Printing (Singapore) under the supervision of
MRM Graphics, Winslow, Buckinghamshire, UK

Contents

Introduction

When I was asked if I would write an introduction to this book I jumped at the chance. Having worked for *The Router* magazine, first as a freelance writer and reviewer, more recently as Acting Editor and now Consulting Editor, I have known Bob Wearing's output as a woodworking writer for a long time. We have chatted often and I have been struck by his depth of knowledge and experience.

He has always drawn great inspiration for his ideas and solutions from problems presented to him by woodworking students at Shrewsbury College and, latterly, Bob's fertile mind has brought us elegantly simple solutions to common routing needs within the pages of *The Router*. He understands perfectly the old adage that the simplest ideas are the best.

I would say there are two truisms about using the router, first, it is nothing without cutters, because it would otherwise have no reason to exist. Second, the router must be used with proper control. The better the degree of control you have over machine and cutter, the better the result. Bob Wearing's jigs and invaluable advice all conspire to make this laudable aim perfectly possible for the beginner or average router user. Indeed, I have learnt a lot from his articles myself. No-one could forget the umpteen varieties of the infamous 'levelling foot', for example; an unassumingly simple device which can facilitate many different operations.

There is much more to be found within the pages of this book, so dip in and discover the answers to your everyday machining difficulties. Keep this book on your workshop reference shelf, ready to hand. On behalf of GMC Publications, may I take the opportunity to thank all of you who have invested in this book, I know you will not be disappointed.

Anthony Bailey

Anthony Bailey
interviews
highly regarded
woodworker
and teacher
Bob Wearing

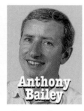

BOB WEARING is one of most prolific writers on routing, with his fascinating articles covering all kinds of simple jigs which extend the range and precision of routers. It seemed only right that we should ask Bob to enter the spotlight of *My Router Workshop* – to find out makes him tick!

College days

Bob went to school just before World War II, which he then went through as a soldier in the old Indian Army of the British Raj. "Like so many who found themselves de-mobbed after the war, I was faced with the difficulty of finding myself a career. I wasn't entitled to a grant as my education hadn't been interrupted by the War, so I spoke to my old headmaster, who after studying my school records (in which I had shone at woodworking), his brief and succinct answer was – go to Loughborough College, nowhere else – they'll make a craftsman of you".

"That was one of life's turning points. I made a test piece in the garden shed with what tools I happened to have, and took it with me for the interview. In spite of enormous competition, I was in! Joining

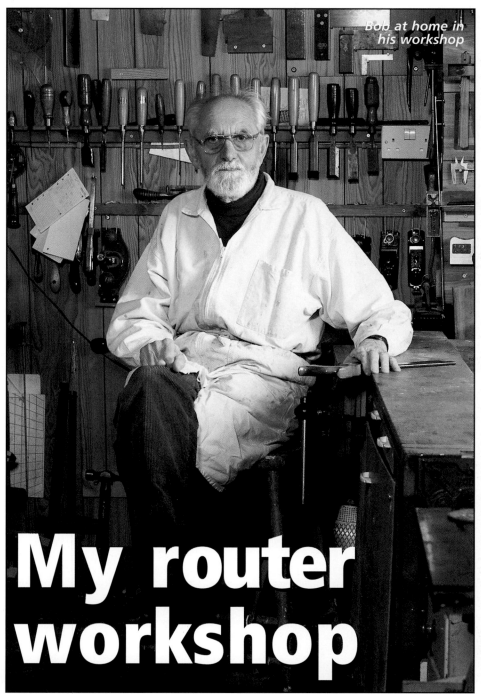

Bob at home in his workshop

My router workshop

A home-made router table with Bosch and Elu routers

scores of ex-servicemen, ranging from a brigadier to modest aircraftsmen".

It was the right place, at the right time and with the right people. There was Edward Barnsley, the century's outstanding designer, Cecil Cough the master craftsman, and Ockenden, the organiser who made it all run so easily.

Master classes

After an extra diploma year, Bob was invited to set up workshops at Wrekin College in Shropshire, a middle-grade public school, then fully boarding. The hours were long, a 56 hour week plus what he took home, but there were compensations.

"There was no local authority breathing down my neck and telling me what I couldn't do. There was generous funding, with occasional extras for projects if I could make a good case. Above all there

were very supportive parents prepared to foot the bill for quality timber!"

As well as teaching O and A levels, the workshops were open whenever there was leisure time in the afternoons. This meant that really keen pupils could sometimes clock up 10 hours a week. "Living on the spot meant that I had the use of a large well-equipped workshop throughout the holidays. So much space has tended to make me very untidy, which I struggle to overcome in my own workshop".

On leaving Wrekin, Bob was invited to the Fine Furniture Course run by John Price, another Loughborough man, at the School of Art in Shrewsbury. This was fascinating though demanding work which continued until John's retirement, when teaching ended. For some years previously Bob had run the Woodturning course in Leeds and York for the College of Craft

▲ *Overhead routing with the small Bosch router in an old Wolf drill stand. Note the adjustable fence with chip extraction*

▲ *A miniature combination machine in set up for morticing*

Education's Summer School. This was a two week residential course so quite a lot could be achieved.

"So much space has tended to make me very untidy"

Workshop in Wem

"Before I retired I gave up my college house and bought two small 1790 town houses in the small market town of Wem". An immense amount of work was involved in joining these together and making them safe, efficient and comfortable, while living in them at the same time. Across a narrow yard were two brick built outside toilets and wash-houses. These knocked together to make a long narrow workshop, very

comfortable for a one-man workshop.

Woodwork has two thirds of the space and metalwork, including its lathe, one third. An assembly area struggles hard to exist, without much success. Water is laid on and heating is by balanced flue gas. Calor gas bottles for forging and brazing live outside, only coming in when needed. The building itself is a brick lean-to, quite high at the back, giving good timber storage space. A ring main gives plenty of power points and the workshop has its own isolator switch. Bob changed the door to open outwards, giving that bit more working space – a useful tip.

"The roof is insulated and the windows double-glazed. This makes it very snug and limits the noise too. The shop is too narrow to take a man-size dust extractor and me. I recently replaced a burnt-out machine with the Axminster WV100. I find this excellent value and very effec-

tive. I also have a Microclean 400 air filter which does keep the air clean, and runs from a time switch".

The house provides a study and a studio/darkroom and there are two good ironmonger/tool shops just moments away.

"I have always done more teaching of woodwork than making. Most of my domestic furniture has come from my workshop. The proportions of the shop preclude large machinery and this is one reason why I have never considered a combination machine". The machines are individual and small, though all are quite adequate for cabinet work.

Bob has an 8in sawbench – "I wish it was a 10in" – a very useful 12in disc sander, with dust extraction which he constructed, a Eumenia radial arm saw, "a grand little machine" which is kept solely for crosscutting and dimension sawing.

"A small Record bandsaw came to me

▼ *Examples of Bob's ingenuity, including sub-bases for angled routing*

▼ *Sub-bases and fences for repetition grooving*

Routers

An original blue Bosch POF router is mounted in a wheel-out cabinet. It hangs from an aluminium plate let in flush with an MDF top, in spite of its age it still delivers. Another Bosch POF is occasionally mounted as an overhead router in an old heavy Wolf drill stand. It is sometimes useful to see the work actually going on.

There is also an Elu 96E and innumerable jigs. Bob, like most of our other victims in the spotlight, doesn't have lots of routers, which should give plenty of comfort to

▼ *The foot switch, depth gauge and depth adjuster – the locking nut is essential*

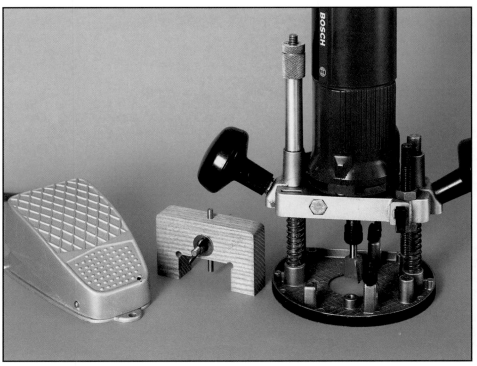

unexpectedly. I find this quite handy; it does all the shaped work which I need. The Record lathe is newish and mounted on my own iron stand, bolted to both floor and wall, so it is steady as a rock".

The Elu 8in planer/thicknesser has served Bob well, without a hitch since the day he bought it. Its slot-morticing attachment has hardly ever been used, the Multico morticer being far better for cabinetmaking and no trouble at all. "An old pre-war hand-cranked drilling machine is fitted permanently for countersinking" says Bob. "This is a very useful idea, so if you see one at a car boot sale or the like, snap it up".

"I have always done more teaching of woodwork than making"

many readers who might feel under-equipped in this area. What is self evident is that Bob manages to do a lot with the few routers he has, and to make this point we move swiftly on to Bob Wearing's jigs.

Jigs

Anyone reading Bob's articles in *The Router* knows just how clever and prolific his inventive mind really is. From the 'Bob Wearing levelling foot' to the the more sophisticated 'Mini Combination Machine', he has thought of just about every device you can make and fit to the average small router.

"The combination machine does morticing, but it will also thickness, rebate and do grooving and moulding. It just needs a little care and ingenuity and you come up with the miniature version of a full size machine!"

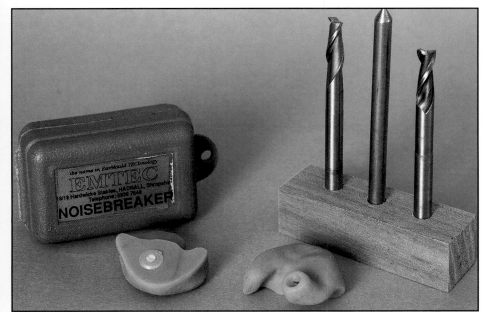

◀*Ear defenders, a ¼in locating point, and two ¼in milling cutters, good for cutting deep mortices*

▲ *A variety of cutters, including straight, dovetail and bearing-guided cutters. The alloy guidebushes are an older Bosch pattern*

Another Bob favourite is the overhead router. Simple refinements to the home-made bed allow easy fence adjustment and the use of ash spring fingers, again fully adjustable, make routing easy and safe with chatter-free cutting.

Gadgets

"I don't own lots of ready-made gadgets, though there are a number of things, including safety aids, which your readers might find interesting. For example, the Emtec 'Noisebreakers'. These superb ear defenders are inconspicuous and let me clearly hear the phone, while giving protection against damaging noises – shooters use them".

"The Vanguard Routing Rods which I have mentioned before in the magazine have a hundred uses because, unlike conventional rods, they take washers and butterfly nuts at each end, allowing the fixing-on of levelling feet, ski's and fences. The V-groove push stick allows safe machining, with the 'V' pushing against the corner of a workpiece, eliminating the need for a second pushstick. I wouldn't be without the foot switch, it leaves both my hands free to control the work".

The router setting depth gauge gives precise cutter settings in the table, whilst the depth adjuster is very useful for table work too.

Cutters

"I have all the usual standard cutters that anyone would own" says Bob. "However as I do quite bit of morticing I find ¼in engineers' milling cutters very effective, because they permit deeper cutting than standard router cutters. The shank enters the hole once the the fluted section has done its work. I don't have any great need for fancy cutters, apart from anything else I don't have a large router to use them in!"

I asked Bob how long he had been writing for woodworking magazines. "If my memory serves me right it was in the 1950's for *The Woodworker,* when it was under the complete and all–embracing control of the great Charles Hayward. He ran it virtually singled-handed, quite a feat no-one has achieved since, and there are all his books on woodworking too, a truly legendary figure who has inspired many people to take up woodworking".

Finally, I wanted to know if there was anything Bob dislikes about woodworking. "Perhaps the only thing is the many editors pressuring me to deliver articles to them all the time!" We would like to say – sorry Bob, you really are much too useful, readers and pupils everywhere have learnt a tremendous amount from you!

Bob's workshop, as tidy as it's ever been!

Small workpiece held in the bench vice, showing the router lipping

Routing in the vice

Turn your vice into a router jig with this simple modification

THIS IS probably the cheapest, and certainly one of the simplest and most useful, routing aids.

The holding of small components for routing is always a problem: they are dangerous when handled on a router table and, of course, freehand routing is impracticable as there is not enough surface on which to run the router. Equally, using a fence is extremely awkward, if not impossible, without introducing a longer register surface for it to follow.

Simple adaption

By using a simple adaption to a conventional woodworking vice it is possible to increase the bearing surface for the router. This will allow small items to be safely gripped and routed, and greatly increase accuracy.

It is assumed that your vice has a wooden cheek fitted to the outer, moving, jaw, and that this cheek is level with the surface of the bench. A hardwood lipping is simply glued to the top of this cheek, thus providing more support for the router's base. This lipping should be fitted to extend beyond the outer face of the vice casting by, say, 6mm (1/4in) or so, and should initially be slightly

> "Now the workpiece is ready for various operations such as grooving, moulding, or even morticing, all guided accurately by the router's fence running on the extended cheek"

Routing a groove in a small component, using the lipping

proud of the bench top. Once fitted, the lipping is trimmed level with the bench's surface with a hand plane.

Parallel trim

When this has been done, set up the router with its fence running along the inner face of the cheek. With a straight, two-flute cutter take a few light cuts from the outer edge of the lipping; this will now be truly parallel to the inside of the jaw – and therefore parallel to any workpiece held in the vice.

In use

To use the newly modified vice cheek as a router guide, grip the workpiece lightly in the vice, leaving it slightly proud of the bench top. With a flat block of board material push the workpiece down to the top of the vice jaws, then fully tighten.

Now the workpiece is

ready for various operations such as grooving, moulding, or even morticing, all guided accurately by the router's fence running on the extended cheek.

The lipping may be left in place permanently as it will not interfere with the normal use of the vice.

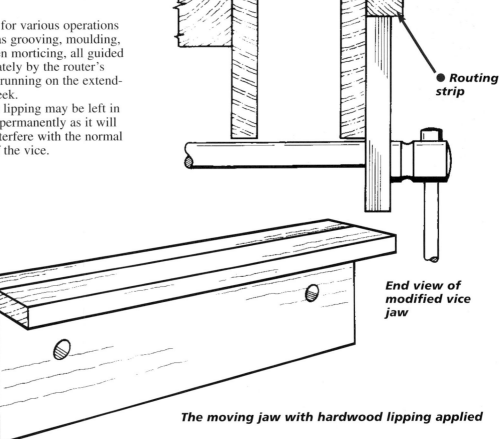

● Routing strip

End view of modified vice jaw

The moving jaw with hardwood lipping applied

Photo 1 The Bob
Wearing levelling foot

The levelling foot

Support an unstable router set-up with this leveller

Any operation where only half of the small router base is settled on the workpiece is inclined to be hazardous. A moment's lack of concentration can cause the router to tilt over, spoiling the work.

The levelling foot device I have designed supports an unstable router set-up and renders this unwelcome rocking impossible, *see photo 1*.

The flexibility of the bar and foot design permits the construction of a number of different feet, aids and appliances, and I find this versatile device amongst the most useful and economical accessories for the router. No doubt readers will find even more applications.

Accessory bars

The majority of routers take accessory bars of $^5/_{16}$in, which is almost indistinguishable from 8mm. To make this levelling device, a pair of special bars will be required, *see fig 1*.

They can be obtained premade from Vanguard Cutting Tools in Sheffield for about £5 including VAT and delivery per pair (see Appendix, page 102, for further details).

Levelling foot

Once a pair of bars has been obtained a hardwood foot can be produced, *see fig 2*. The foot fits on the narrower section of the bars, is held firmly to the shoulder with a wing nut and sandwiched between two washers. Sizes for the foot are merely suggestions as it can be made to suit any type of project.

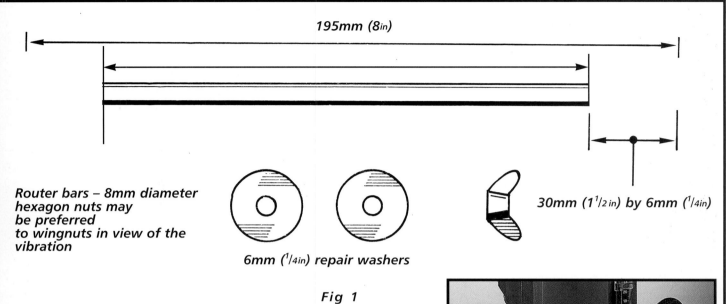

195mm (8in)

Router bars – 8mm diameter hexagon nuts may be preferred to wingnuts in view of the vibration

6mm (¹/₄in) repair washers

30mm (1¹/₂in) by 6mm (¹/₄in)

Fig 1

6¹/₂ (165)

¹/₄BSW or M8

8mm or ⁵/₁₆in (to suit router)

To suit router

⁷/₈ (22)

60mm (2¹/₂in)

6mm (¹/₄in)

Left – Routed slot
Right – Sawn and built up slot

150mm (6in)

Fig 2

Photo 2 Drop the foot into place for tenoning

"I find this versatile device amongst the most useful and economical accessories for the router"

The slots can either be routed in or sawn, in which case a strip of wood is applied to the edge to close the gaps. Make the slots a shade over 6mm (¹/₄in) to allow for a slight adjustment on the bars.

The slots in the foot should be the same distance apart as the holes in the baseplate of the router. It is not easy to measure between the centres of holes so a useful tip is to measure from the left-hand side of one hole to the left-hand side of the other.

This is easily measured and is the same distance as between centres.

In use
To form tenons or half lap joints set up the bars in the router and lock them in place. Fit the levelling foot on the bars and spin up the wing nuts so they are finger tight only.

Stand the router on the workpiece then slacken the wing nuts to allow the levelling foot to drop to the bench top. Secure the wing nuts so the router now has a stable support to run on, *see photo 2*.

Mark the positions of the tenons on the workpieces, cramp one firmly to the bench top then saw a cut on the shoulder line just short of the required depth to create the shoulder of the tenon.

Fit the chosen cutter into the router — a fairly large diameter one will make the job of tenoning quicker. Set the depth of cut approximately, then proceed to remove the waste in a series of cuts, finishing with a fine cut. Turn the workpiece over and

repeat the process of removing waste wood, then try the tenon in its mortice to check it for a good fit. Make any adjustments to depth you require to gain a snug fit, then set the depth stop.

Doing this setting up process on a spare piece of wood the same dimensions as the workpieces is a good idea.

With the router set up, tenons can be produced on all the remaining components.

Router rods are now even more useful, having a thread on each end.

A fence for the levelling foot

The lesson on routing bars continues with an explanation of how to make a fence for a levelling foot

As time goes on I discover more and more uses for my router bars. These fit any router baseplate, and were originally designed for the levelling foot already featured.

Some of the cutters designed for edge work — mouldings, rebates and grooves — are fitted with a bearing which enables them to be used without any sort of fence apart from the bearing itself. This makes them

very convenient and easy to use, but the position of the cut is fixed and only the depth of cut can be altered.

Cuts often have to be made in more specific places where a bearing attached to a cutter is no help. Cutters without a guide bearing are not constrained by a fixed position, and so will need a fence of some sort to position the cut accurately.

For these jobs a sturdy fence is essential.

The router's own fence cannot be used in many instances, but the problem can be quickly solved as one can easily be fitted to my levelling foot design instead.

Levelling foot fence

First find a small piece of suitable hardwood, the same length as the levelling foot and about 12mm (¹/₂in) thick. Make the width about the same size as the distance

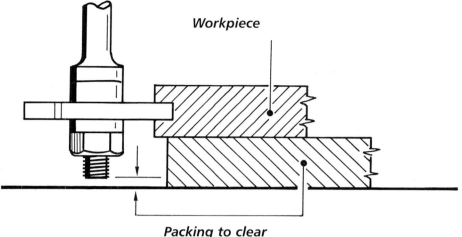

Workpiece

Packing to clear
bench top

Fence for levelling foot ▲ ▶

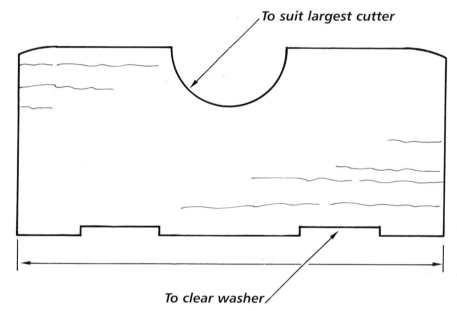

To suit largest cutter

To clear washer

B Working a rebate with a plain ▶
cutter and the fence

from the edge of the router's baseplate to its centre.

In the centre of one edge of the fence cut out a space for the cutter; this cut-out must be quite large if a slotting cutter is to be used. Fences can be made with cut-outs to suit individual cutters, or make an all-purpose model with a cut-out to fit your largest cutter. To accommodate the large washers, two shallow cavities will be needed on the other edge of the fence where it attaches to the levelling foot.

Drill and countersink a couple of holes in the bottom edge of the levelling foot; these are for attaching the fence.

Finally, screw the two components together and fix them to the router rods.

Using the fence

In use, the combined levelling leg and fence provide a stable platform as well as the means to position the cutter accurately. With some types of cutter, particularly arbor-mounted disc cutters, the workpiece may have to be placed on top of a piece of packing to give the end of the cutter clearance from the benchtop.

Availability

Router rods, to my own specifications, are now manufactured, and are available from Vanguard Cutting Tools, Sheffield (see the Appendix, page 102, for further details).

The cost for the pair, available in either 8 or 10mm sizes, is about £5, inclusive of VAT, postage and packing — a trouser pocket rather than cheque book price; allow seven working days for delivery.

Edge jointing

How to make a jointing board for use with a router

AT some time or another the need to widen a surface by edge-jointing will arise. For those without a planer or jointer, or lacking the experience to make a good job of hand-jointing – or simply when time is of the essence – help is at hand in the form of the versatile router.

Basically all that is required is a jointing board. This consists of two boards forming a flat machining bed on which the router and the work sit, with a slot to take the cutter. A separate fence is clamped to the assembly.

The length of the board depends on the size of work contemplated; for width, the dimensions given, *see below*, are generally suitable.

Method of work

Clamp on the first piece to be jointed, true face upwards. If the component is small, *see photo*, hold it with several strips of double-sided tape. This first piece must overhang the central gap by, say, 6mm (¼in) or a little less.

Similarly, fix the second workpiece, true face down, but this time just clear of the gap; its sole purpose, so far, is to keep the router level.

Set up the router without a side fence and fit a good quality TCT straight cutter with a cutting length greater than the thickness of the workpiece; 12.5mm (½in) diameter or greater is quite suitable.

Clamp on the fence so that the router, when its baseplate is run along it, will take a cut no greater than 3mm (⅛in), preferably less. Switch on and traverse from right to left.

Running a pencil line along the edge is helpful; even if the router should drift away from the fence, leaving pencil marks, no harm is done. Have another go and all will be well.

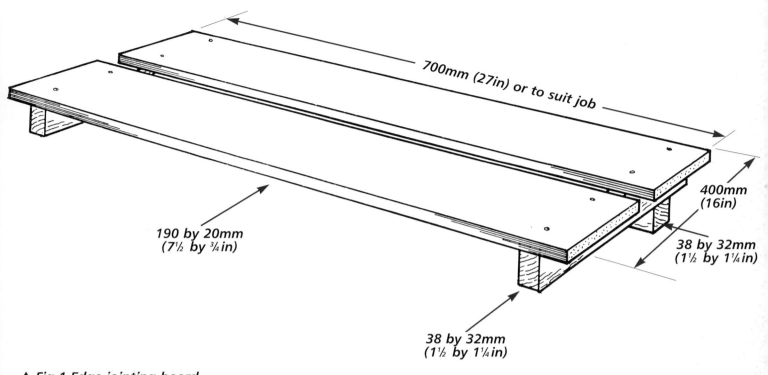

700mm (27in) or to suit job

400mm
(16in)

190 by 20mm
(7½ by ¾in)

38 by 32mm
(1½ by 1¼in)

38 by 32mm
(1½ by 1¼in)

▲ Fig 1 Edge jointing board

Board set up for second cut

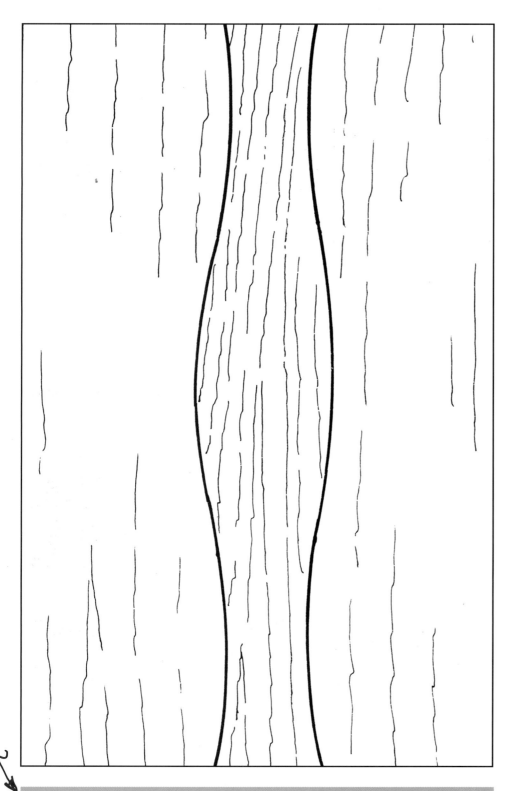

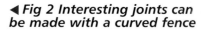
◀ *Fig 2 Interesting joints can be made with a curved fence*

"If there is any unsquareness between router base and cutter, try cramping one workpiece with its true face up and the other with its true face down"

Second cut

The first workpiece and the fence must not be disturbed. Release the uncut piece and secure it over the gap. To obtain a convenient gap between the two components, turn the router bit so that the actual cutting edges are clear of the wood, then move in the second piece until it touches the cutter at both ends and fix it firmly.

Again, traverse the router along the fence, this time from left to right. The joint is now complete. In the event of the router drifting away from the fence, move the workpiece in a little more and traverse the router again.

Note that the cut can only be made at full depth; two cuts with a short router cutter will not work.

If there is any unsquareness between router base and cutter, try clamping one workpiece with its true face up and the other with its true face down. To exaggerate, this action will cut one board at 91° and the other at 89°, the combination being 180°, i.e. flat.

Variation

A router with a circular baseplate run along a curved fence could be used in this way to create an interesting joint, particularly when contrasting woods or components with very differing grain patterns are jointed.

Construction

MDF is coming under increasing criticism on health grounds and may have a tendency to sag in length. Make the edge-jointing board from two pieces of good quality multi-ply or blockboard. Screw these onto two battens, adding extra battens if a longer board is needed and leaving a space between them of about 25mm (1in). Add a lengthwise batten to act as a gripping piece in the vice. Finally, make a fence.

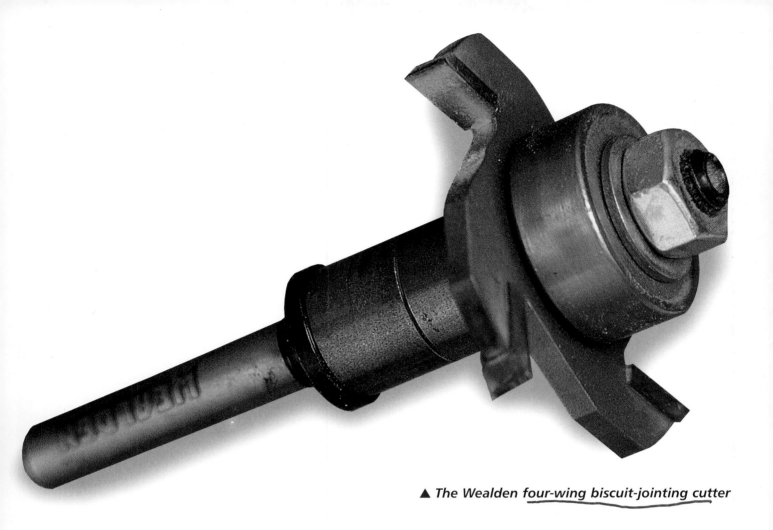

▲ *The Wealden four-wing biscuit-jointing cutter*

Biscuit jointing

Looking at the biscuit jointer and how this useful tool can be used with a router

THE biscuit jointer, costing between £120 and £470, is now firmly established as a power tool. Although it is often found in busy professional workshops, many smaller concerns and skilled amateurs may have reservations about it, however, being uncertain whether they will have either the use for it, or the funds to buy one.

By far the most common use for biscuit-jointing is in forming an edge joint when joining boards together to create a wider one.

Not much more is required than the accurate lining up of edges. Perfect joints can then be made with a router fitted with a biscuit-jointing cutter.

Biscuit-jointing cutters are available with either two or four wings, depending on the manufacturer. Different sized bearings can be fitted to the arbor for setting the depth of cut. On some cutters the bearing can be set either above the cutter, for thin workpieces, or below it for thicker ones.

I use The Wealden Tool Company's biscuit-jointing cutter kit. Well thought out, it consists of a 4-wing 4mm-thick cutter,

spacing washers to locate the cutter accurately and three bearings matching the three sizes of biscuit – small, 0, medium, 10 and large, 20.

Arbors are available with ¼, ⅜ or ½in shanks. You do not have to buy the complete set as all the items can be bought separately.

My biscuits come from **Axminster Power Tools Centre**, Chard Street, Axminster, Devon EX13 5DZ, Freephone 0800 371822. A small assorted pack of 500 and one-size packs of 1000 are also available.

▲Two wing cutters with different sized bearings fitted

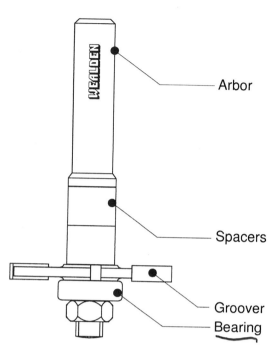

Arbor

Spacers

Groover
Bearing

▲ Anatomy of a router biscuit-jointing cutter

▶ Note the two pencil marks. The cutter is moved from one to the other to obtain the correct slot length

▼ Biscuits come in three sizes. Various bearings fitted to the arbor enable the correct depth for each biscuit slot to be cut

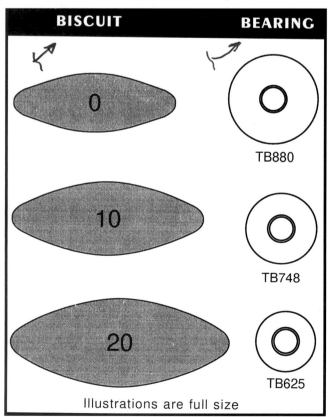

BISCUIT	BEARING
0	TB880
10	TB748
20	TB625

Illustrations are full size

"An accurate length of slot is not really important, but being of a pedantic nature I mark further lines 10mm (³⁄₈in) on each side of the centre line"

Alternative techniques

It occurred to me that the router could be used in one of three ways: overhead routing, in a routing table or freehand, *see below*.

With any type of biscuit-jointing, marking out is simple. Having created good joint faces on the boards, lay the two together and mark the centre line of the slot across both.

An accurate length of slot is not really important, but being of a pedantic nature I mark further lines 10mm (³⁄₈in) on each side of the centre line, i.e. 19mm (³⁄₄in) included. This is for the No. 10 biscuit, so will differ for Nos. 0 and 20.

Overhead routing

This calls for a wooden base plate with a hole bored and elongated to accept the end of the arbor. Set up the cutter on the arbor, locating the spacers to position it conveniently for the thickness of the job.

Gluing tip

Glue the joint first and the biscuits last. If biscuits are permitted to stand about wet for any appreciable length of time they will swell and be difficult to insert.

▲ Overhead biscuit-jointing with a small Bosch router set up in drill stand

"Adjust the cutter height to the centre of the workpiece. This position is not critical but, being a niggler, I have to have it truly central"

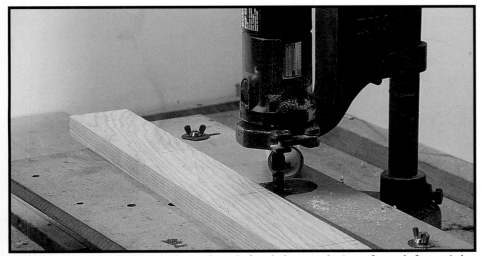

▲ With the router mounted overhead, feed the workpiece from left to right

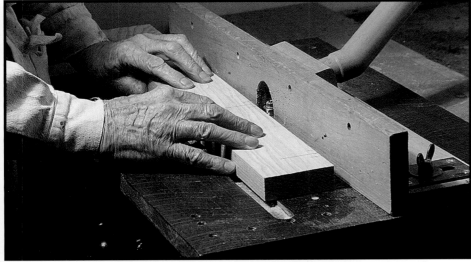

▲ The router inverted in a workshop-built routing table means the feed direction is right to left

Though possibly not essential, I find it convenient to fix a fence, with a notch cut out for the cutter. The fence is cramped so that the chosen bearing projects minutely in front of its working face.

Make sure that the router's base-plate, fence and cutter in its collet are all firmly held.

Adjust the cutter height to the centre of the workpiece. This position is not critical but, being a niggler, I have to have it truly central. Really, as long as all the 'true' faces of the timber are placed either up or down, a level joint will be obtained.

Feed in the workpiece with one line pointing to the centre of the arbor. The traverse must be made against the rotation of the cutter. Looking from above, the direction of the cutter is clockwise, so the movement of the workpiece is from left to right.

Keeping fingers well away from the cutter, maintain a firm downward pressure on the workpiece. Withdraw it when the second line is reached.

Router table

The hole in the table plate must be large enough for the cutter to pass through. Make sure that the cutter is very firmly held in the collet and the router solidly mounted in the table.

The gap in the table's fence should be set to support the work while providing the cutter with some clearance.

Set the fence so that the bearing projects very slightly in front of its working face, and adjust the cutter height to the centre of the workpiece.

Mark out the biscuit positions and feed in as described for the overhead router. Feed the workpiece against the cutter's direction of rotation. Looked at from above, this is anti-clockwise, so feed from right to left.

With care, biscuit slots can be cut in the end-grain on, for example, the rails of a flat frame. The close gap in the fence will help to support the workpiece.

They can also be machined on mitres in a wide, flat frame. In both cases, use the largest biscuit possible. If the workpiece is thick enough, a pair of biscuits can be fitted.

Freehand routing

Using a router freehand for biscuit-jointing can be somewhat precarious because less than half of the router base bears on the workpiece.

This stability problem can be easily overcome by adding a levelling foot to the router.

Fit the bars on the router and clamp them tightly. Stand the router on the workpiece, drop the levelling foot to the benchtop and clamp it in place, then slide the foot close to the baseplate and clamp it tight.

Fit the biscuit-jointing cutter into the router and plunge it down so it is positioned in the centre of the workpiece, then lock the plunge. If the tip of the arbor hits the benchtop, lift the workpiece by inserting a scrap of plywood or multi-ply under it, and re-adjust the levelling foot.

▲ *The close gap in the fence helps to support narrow workpieces when jointed on the ends*

▲ *Freehand routing with the Levelling Foot*

"With care, biscuit slots can be cut in the end-grain on, for example, the rails of a flat frame"

▲ *Levelling Foot will permit safe freehand biscuit-jointing*

Test the cut on an offcut of the same thickness as the job.

Mark out as previously described, and ensure that the workpiece is held firmly to the benchtop while biscuit-jointing. Feed in the cutter, traversing from left to right while maintaining a firm downward pressure on the router.

Sweet favourite

I was most pleasantly surprised by the sweetness of the cutting action, making this my favourite of the three methods described. When the components are long, wide or heavy, this becomes the most practical method

Levelling foot bars are now manufactured to my specification by **Vanguard Cutting Tools**, Sheffield (see Appendix, page 102). Router Rods cost about £5 for the 8mm (⅜in) size and £5.50 for the 10mm size, including VAT, postage and packing.

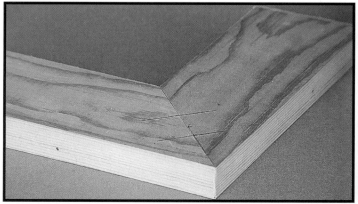

▲ *Inserting biscuits into mitre joints is also possible with care*

▲*Clamp workpieces down securely before jointing*

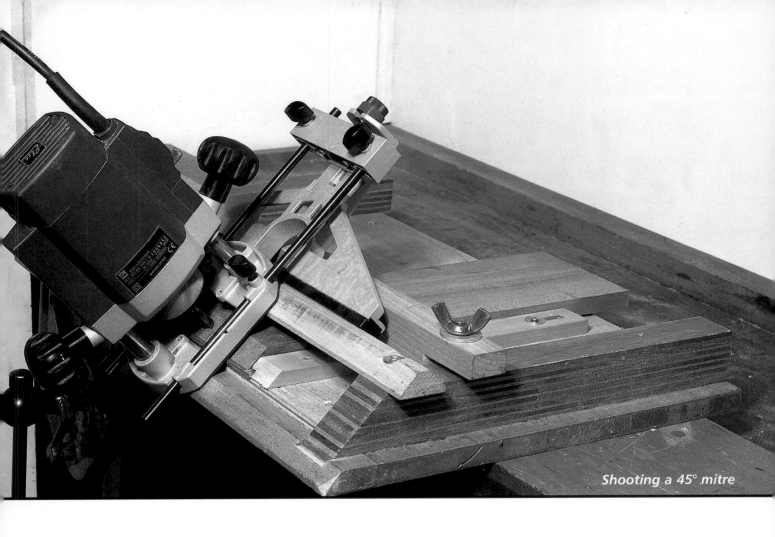

Shooting a 45° mitre

Router shooting board for 45°

How to make shooting boards for a router to cut accurately at a 45° angle

IT is absurd to have available the power of the router and not to exploit it to the full. Here is an opportunity to do just that, to accurately rout a 45° angle on the edge of a board. The construction of the shooting board jig is quite straightforward, and being well made it will last a lifetime.

The router shooting board 45°

Cut the baseboard to size – I made mine 560 by 38mm (22 by 1½in). It is best not to use solid wood unless it's well seasoned because of the risk of warping – in preference use 19mm (¾in) multi-ply which is a good stable material, or alternatively blockboard or MDF.

Prepare a hardwood lipping, slightly thicker than the sheet material. Glue this on the long edge using a 6mm (¼in) plywood loose tongue. The router will cut the grooves for this perfectly. If both components are grooved centrally, the lipping will be slightly proud either side – plane this off so that it is flush.

Now machine a 45° bevel on the lipping, using a table or radial arm saw or even a hand plane. Check the angle with the bevel set from a set square or combination-square.

"Do not use solid wood unless it is well seasoned because of the risk of warping"

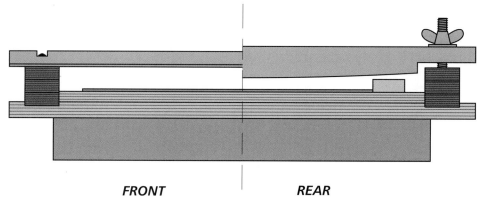

FRONT   **REAR**

"Thoroughly tighten the screws – the positioning of these is important to avoid ending up with a twisted box"

▲ *Front and rear view of the 45°
shooting jig*

▶ *Mark the inside length of the 45° angles
on a board to help setting the depth of cut*

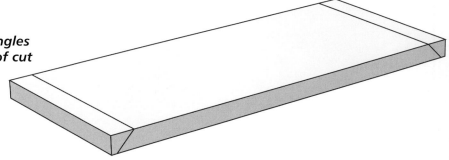

Screw the vice gripping strip onto the baseboard. Fix this on early as it is a help when working some of the processes which follow.

Check that both ends of the baseboard are square to the hardwood lipping then rout a housing (dado) for the end-blocks. This should be positioned in from each end, and 3mm (⅛in) deep by 41mm (1⅝in) wide.

The two end-blocks are built up from layers of multi-ply rather than solid wood since any shrinkage will result in the 45° angle decreasing. Make these blocks to width, shaving by shaving, and fit them tightly into their housing. When you're satisfied that they fit well, cut one end to 45° and the other end to length, and square. These end blocks can now be glued and screwed into place, noting that the 45° face is set back slightly from the hardwood lipping runner.

From another piece of hardwood prepare

"When completely satisfied tighten the screws firmly taking care not to knock the tool out of adjustment"

the top runner with a 45° angle on either side. Cut a small housing at each end for a washer and drill an oversize hole for the fixing screws. Screw it in place then check the angle. When completely satisfied tighten the screws firmly taking care not to knock the

tool out of adjustment. Test by routing two mitres, assembling them and checking the resulting angle with a try square.

The top runner must be set up very precisely since any error will be multiplied by 8, i.e. an almost undetectable error of ¼° will amount to 2° when the fourth joint closes.

Add a platform of 19mm (¾in) plywood between the two end-blocks. The front angle can be left square. This is screwed into place with the front edge clear of the 45° angle.

The clamp bar is made of a dense hardwood such as beech. It is notched loosely at each end and the bottom surface is very slightly curved to allow it to pull up tight. For the clamping screws you can use lengths of 12.7mm (½in) threaded rod with the end blocks drilled and tapped. Alternatively use bolts that go right through the assembly, the baseboard being counterbored for their heads. Roofing bolts are fine for this since their heads are thin. The clamp bar is drilled to house these screws. An oversize hole of 14mm permits easy movement.

If you like, the curved surface of the clamp bar can be faced with glasspaper. Glue on a piece that is larger than the surface. When it's dry, score round it with an awl or pointed implement. The excess will then tear off easily.

For an added refinement, fit a pair of weak coil springs on the clamp screws between the clamp bar and end-blocks. These will keep the bar raised when feeding in the workpiece.

▼ *A view of the jig showing construction*

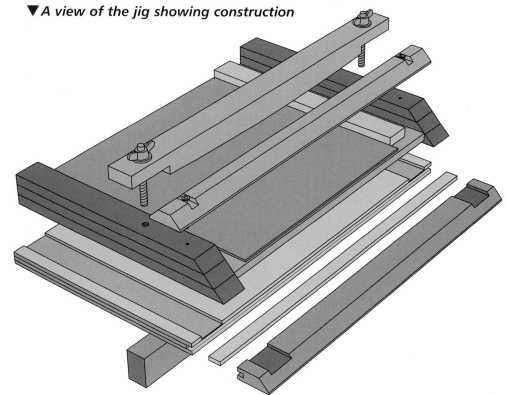

Method of Work

Cut the pieces, that will take the 45° angle, slightly over length on a table or radial arm saw fitted with a suitable stop. Then mark the inside length of the 45° angle on both ends of one of the pieces.

Next screw a locating strip on to the baseboard of the jig. Its position will depend on the width of the workpiece, which will generally be clamped roughly in the centre of the jig.

Lay a flat off-cut across the two runners and with a large set square check that the locating strip is square to it. A set square will be more accurate than some try-squares. Thoroughly tighten the screws – the positioning of these is important to avoid ending up with a twisted box.

Lay a scrap of hardboard or plywood under the workpiece to prevent damage to the shooting board.

Still with the offcut across the runners, push the first workpiece firmly against both this and the locating strip. Clamp firmly.

Set up the router with its largest diameter cutter. For routers taking only ¼in shanks, this will probably be 19mm (¾in). A smaller cutter can be used by sliding the router down the fence bars to take a second cut at

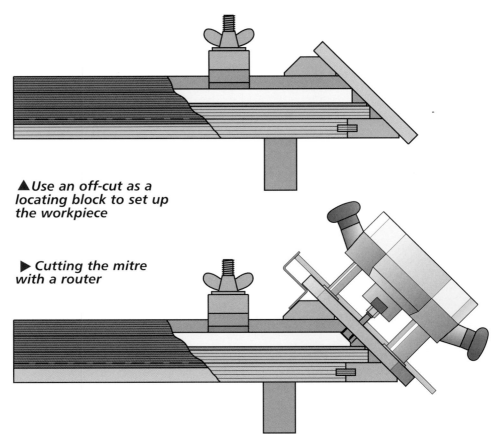

▲ *Use an off-cut as a locating block to set up the workpiece*

▶ *Cutting the mitre with a router*

the same setting. Hang the fence over the top runner and adjust so that the cutter is central over the mitre. Set a small depth of cut then traverse across the workpiece. Increase the cut by stages until the inner length line has been reached. Lock a depth

stop at this setting.

Turn the workpiece round to mitre the other end. Set up and cramp in the same way. Take several cuts, finishing up with the depth stop engaged. All pieces initially sawn to the same length, will now be identical.

The completed shooting board

Router shooting board for 90°

How to make router shooting boards to accurately rout 90° edges

IT is absurd to have available the power of the router and not to exploit it to the full. Here is an opportunity to do just that – to take the hard work out of straightening edges and to have a guarantee of accuracy. The construction of the shooting board jig is quite straightforward and, being well made, will last a lifetime.

90° Shooting board

Planing end grain hardwood is not amongst the most pleasant workshop jobs, and the machine planer does not seem to enjoy it either. But the versatile router comes to the rescue – it does the job well, and leaves a fine finish.

Any router will do. A tungsten carbide tipped cutter is recommended, as high speed steel will not last long on end grain. A long fence is also an advantage. If the router does not have this, add a wooden fence.

Freehand routing is impracticable, so a shooting board must be made. Start with the backboard – my sizes are only suggestions, but will cover most work.

Backboard

Preferably use good quality 19mm (¾in) multi-ply – MDF is also suitable, but doubts are beginning to be raised about its safety. Produce the component to size and then rout the slot. Add a hardwood lipping to the backboard and ensure that it has a true edge which is square to the face.

Next, the two end blocks are prepared. They are glued and· screwed in place. The front runner, also of matching hardwood, can then be glued and screwed in place as well. The two runners must be truly parallel. If you have access to a planer you can quickly achieve this – one or two passes will suffice.

"The construction of the shooting board jig is quite straightforward and, being well made, will last a lifetime"

Moveable fence

A movable fence can now be screwed in place, to suit the width of the workpiece. Use round-head woodscrews, through 'repair' washers. Make the holes in the fence oversize to permit fine adjustment.

To check the accuracy of the device, lay a flat board across the runners and use a large draughtsman's set-square between this and the fence, then adjust the fence as necessary. Screw a flat strip behind the backboard, by which the shooting board can be clamped to the bench top.

Clamping

The workpiece can be held in place either by two slim clamps through the slot, gripping a loose wood block behind, or by specially made handscrew-like clamps.

The two clamps are made to the dimensions given. To avoid having to cut threads, tee-nuts are used – these are easily obtainable. Don't hammer them in, as they may go in skew or the threads may damage – pull them in with a

The completed board

"The versatile router comes to the rescue – it does the job well, and leaves a fine finish"

bolt, washer and wood block. The thumbscrews are made by securing wing-nuts to pieces of screwed rod by thin hexagon lock nuts. Screwing two strips to the rear face, *see photo*, will help locate the clamps.

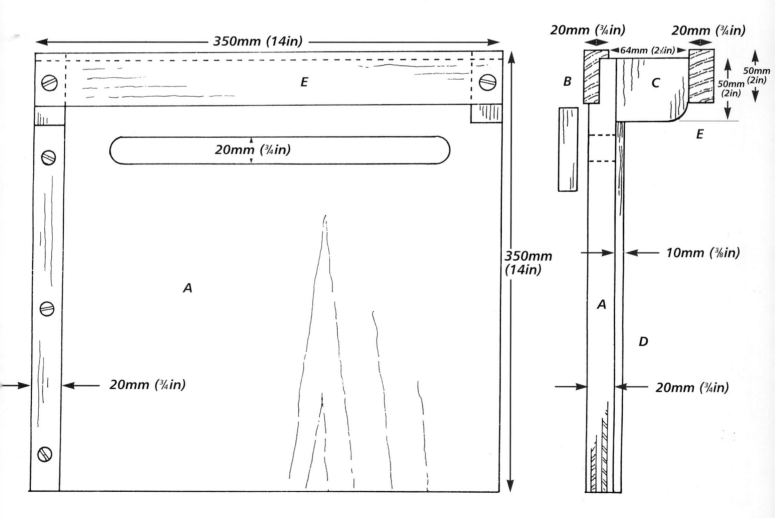

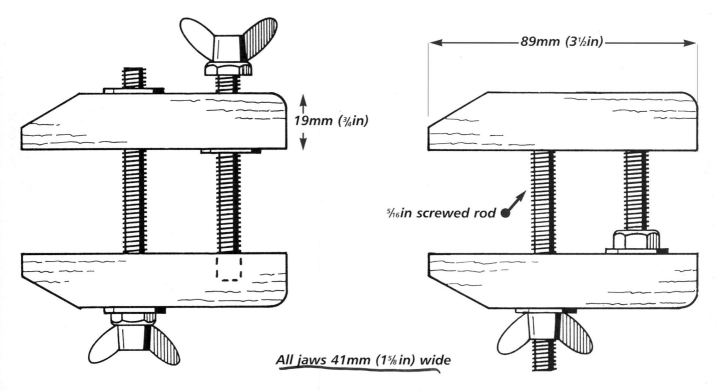

19mm (¾in)

89mm (3½in)

⁵⁄₁₆in screwed rod ●

All jaws 41mm (1⅝in) wide

Rear view of the shooting board showing clamps and guide bars

▲ _Alternative clamps for shooting board_

or until the marked line is reached. Increase the cut by router adjustment. Do not move the workpiece once it has been clamped in place.

The result is a fine finish, dead square in both directions, achieved in moments. No skill is required, and there is no chance of failure! ●

"When cutting on the near face of the workpiece, traverse from left to right, and on the far side, from right to left"

"Tungsten carbide cutters are essential, because end-grain work soon finishes off high speed steel cutters"

▼ _Detail view of the clamps_

Method

Clamp the workpiece to the backboard. Its true edge must be against the fence and its top edge, that is, the edge to be worked, must be just below the working face of the runners. Tungsten carbide cutters are essential, because end-grain work soon finishes off high speed steel cutters.

Fit a plain end cutting bit in the router. Any size except the very small will do, say 6 to 19mm (¼ to ¾in). Fit and adjust the long fence so that the cutter just clears the workpiece at the far side, that is, the backboard, making sure it does not

cut into the runners. When cutting on the near face of the workpiece, traverse from left to right, and on the far side, from right to left. The far cut is controlled by the fence. Nearer cuts are made freehand. Thinner components, of course, are completed in one cut.

Take a series of fine cuts until the whole surface is clean

Routing small circles

How to make a jig for use when routing small circles

MANY routers come with a circle-cutting device. These versions of routers, however, are not designed to cope with either very large radii or very small circles.

Small routed circles are often required for many purposes, such as through-holes for cabling in computer desks. Shallow, circular recesses are another example and these can be used in pieces of furniture for the location of stored items, such as in coin cabinets and collectors' cases. Toymaking is another area where the ability to rout small circles is invaluable, when small wooden wheels for trains, cars and lorries have to be made.

The devices described below will help with all these examples and many more, and I will show you how to make two different types of jig. One is adjustable for varying the size of circles to be routed, *see photo 1*, and the other is fixed. One must be made for each size of circle.

▲ *Fit a set of my router bars to the block on the end of the jig*

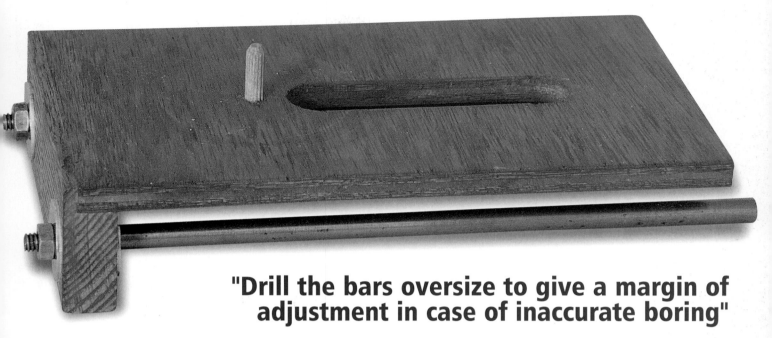

"Drill the bars oversize to give a margin of adjustment in case of inaccurate boring"

Adjustable jig

The adjustable small circle jig is yet another use for my router bars described in earlier issues.

Sizes of the jigs will, of course, depend on the router to be used, but the majority of routers used by amateurs and some professionals have fence bars of 5⁄16in diameter, which for our purposes is indistinguishable from 8mm.

Make a baseboard from 6 or 8mm plywood; it should be about the width of the router's baseplate and about twice as long. Cut a central slot of about 25mm (1in) wide running lengthways on the jig's baseboard, stopping well short either end.

Prepare a hardwood block and drill two holes in it to take the threaded ends of the router bars, *see below*. To do this, measure carefully the distance between the holes on your router's baseplate and transfer this measurement to the block of wood. It is easier to measure from the inside edge of one hole to the outside edge of the other

Slide the router onto the bars to set the diameter of the circle

▲ *A jig that will cut circles of a fixed size is also easy to make*

rather than trying to line up the tape measure, or ruler, with the centre of the holes, and the measurement will be the same. Drill holes in the block for the router bars slightly oversize to give a margin of adjustment in case of inaccurate boring.

Glue the block to the baseboard and, when dry, clean up any excess glue from the joint and finish off by rounding the corners and edges of the jig.

The jig can be pivoted on either a screw or a dowel, the latter being preferable when making wheels which have been pre-bored. Drill a hole in the baseboard on its centre line, for the dowel, *see photo 2*, for the approximate position. This is not critical as the router is moved to create different-sized circles.

Then glue it in place and set the jig aside to dry fully.

In use

Fix the bars in place and slide the router onto them, *see photo 3*, making adjustments to achieve the correct radius for the circle required. If routing a hole, set the router so that it cuts slightly undersize, but if cutting discs set it slightly oversize. This allows for a final fine cut to finish off.

Plunge to the required depth, by stages if this is considerable, and finish with a fine cut of the required diameter. The workpiece needs to be drilled in the exact centre of the required circle; the hole should be a good fit on the pivot dowel, but it should also allow free swivel.

*Router bars are manufactured to my specification by **Vanguard Cutting Tools**, Sheffield (see page 102). The cost for the pair in either 8 or 10mm is about £5, including VAT, postage and packing.*

Fixed size jig

The fixed jig, *see photo 5*, works on the same principle as the adjustable jig, but this time it fixes directly onto the baseplate of the router. Cut a piece of 6 or 8mm plywood slightly larger than the baseplate and mark on it the positions of the mounting holes.

This can be done by poking a pencil through them and making a mark or, if this is not possible, measure the positions of the holes and transfer them onto the plywood.

Drill and countersink them, then drill a larger hole in the centre to allow the cutter to pass through. As before, drill a hole for the dowel pivot and glue in place .

This will need some careful calculation if an exact size of circle is required, and its position will also depend on the size of cutter used.

Fix the jig to the router, drill the work-piece to accommodate the dowel pivot, then carefully rout the circle. As the size of the circle to be cut is fixed it is not possible to set the jig over or undersize to take the small cut to finish off, so small, incremental depth settings are best taken to achieve this.

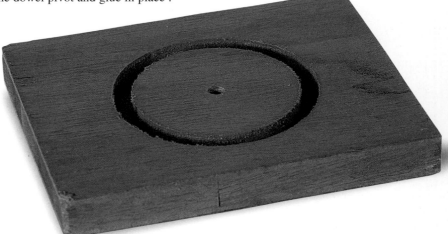

▲ *A routed small circle – for safety hold the centre in position with double-sided tape*

Small circle cutting tips

1. When a central disc of waste is released it may jam or even fly out, dangerously – at least to the workpiece. To prevent this, use double-sided tape to hold down onto some waste material, see photo 6.
2. Cavities which will be seen and polished are best routed using a very short dowel in a shallow hole.
3. Adopt a comfortable stance that will allow a wide arc of the circle to be cut before a new position is adopted.

Any length can be slotted in a vice fitted with a routing lip on the moving jaw

Working short slots

The best advice on producing slots

I OFTEN have to make slots for the various jigs which I make – adjustable components like fences – and if there are any processes for which I bless the router, this is certainly one of them.

In the old days we had to bore a hole at each end, saw out the slot with a padsaw or bowsaw and finish by filing.

The appearance of the portable jigsaw helped, but the job was still tedious; so the router transformed life.

Slotting, of course, is just extra-deep grooving – which would quickly ruin the benchtop, if not protected.

Slots may be required along the length of the component, or across its width, and I discuss both techniques below.

Lengthwise

The requirement for lengthwise slotting is a routing lip on the vice. To make this, glue a strip to the outside face of the moving jaw, sufficiently wide to overhang the metalwork.

Close the vice and plane flush with the benchtop. Now open the vice and run the router fence along the inside face of the moving jaw to take a cut from the out-

"Open the vice and run the router fence along the inside face of the moving jaw to take a cut from the outside edge of the lip"

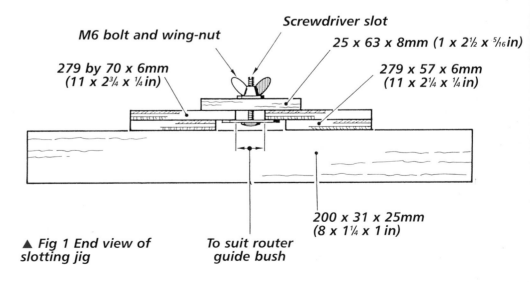

M6 bolt and wing-nut

Screwdriver slot

279 by 70 x 6mm
(11 x 2¾ x ¼ in)

25 x 63 x 8mm (1 x 2½ x ⁵⁄₁₆ in)

279 x 57 x 6mm
(11 x 2¼ x ¼ in)

200 x 31 x 25mm
(8 x 1¼ x 1 in)

▲ Fig 1 End view of slotting jig

To suit router guide bush

Routing a long slot with a small Bosch router

"One length stop terminates the cut and the other gives the start – and also safeguards the vice jaw from accidentally being cut"

On the underside, rout a central groove 1½ by ⅛in (38 by 3mm), then rout through the centre of this at a size that will match your router's guide bush. The bush should slide sweetly in the slot without wobbling or binding.

The plywood is then secured to a batten to keep the jig square to the workpiece and the jig is ready for use with the addition of a pair of endstops to limit the length of the cut.

An alternative method of constructing the jig is to make it from two strips of plywood, *see figs 1 and 2*, which are built up from thinner material and a tie piece arranged at one end. Glue and screw these to a hardwood batten measuring, say, 1½ by 1in (38 by 25mm), making sure that the slot is accurately square to the batten. It is worth undercutting the inside face of the batten so that the jig will sit flat on

side edge of the lip. The lip will now be truly parallel with any workpiece held in the vice.

Grip the workpiece in the vice, flush with the top – although great accuracy here is not important.

Work the slot by running the fence along the routing lip. Take several cuts – the three-way depth stop fitted on some routers comes in useful at this stage.

Longer pieces can be progressively slid through the vice for an accurate finished result.

Crosswise

A jig made from ⅜ or ½in plywood is needed for this process. Make it large enough to suit the baseplate of your router and long enough for the groove lengths you will require.

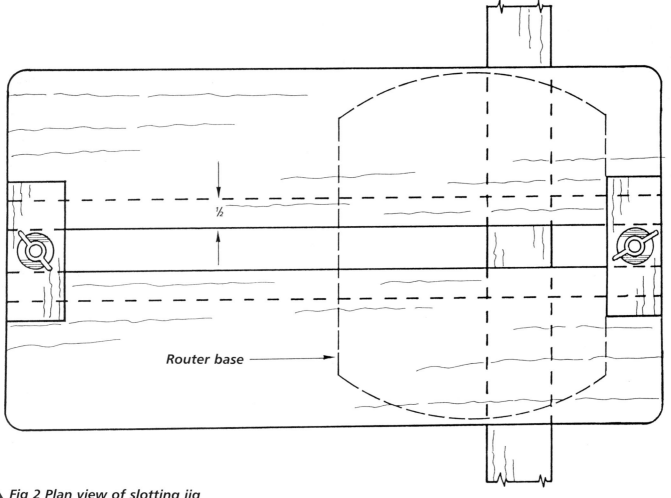

½

Router base

▲ *Fig 2 Plan view of slotting jig*

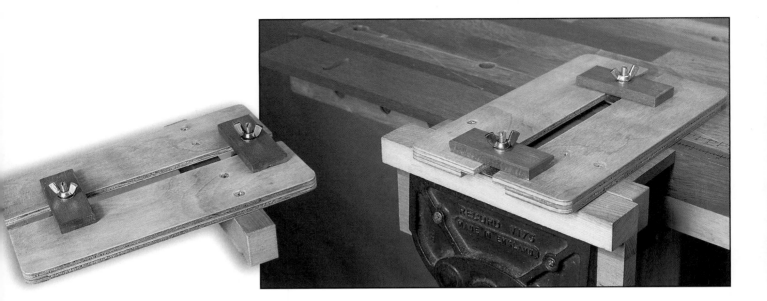

▲ **This jig for cross-grain routing is made from one piece of ply ...**

▲ **... this one is two pieces of ply fixed together with the batten and a tie piece**

the benchtop, *see fig 3*.

Two simple length stops are easily constructed from some scrap material and a selection of bolts, wingnuts and washers that are readily available from any hardware store.

To use either of the jigs simply grip both the jig and the workpiece in the vice. Set the cutter to depth then run the router along the jig with the guide bush in the slot.

One length stop terminates the cut and the other gives the start – and also safeguards the vice jaw from accidentally being cut.

Generally it is wise to make several cuts rather than one complete through cut; this will depend on the power of your router, but whichever way is used a splendidly finished slot will be obtained.

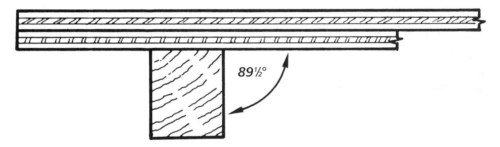

89½°

▲ **Fig 3 Side view of jig showing undercut angle on the batten which will allow it to lie flat on the workbench**

Routing across the grain slot

The keyed mitre joint

How to combine <u>mitre joint</u> and strengthening <u>keys</u> to make a joint good enough for most boxes and carcasses

THE keyed mitre joint is, in effect, two joints: the mitre, which is a notoriously weak joint, and the strengthening keys.

Together, they make a joint approaching in strength the dovetail or the comb joint, which is adequate for most box or carcass jobs.

Early attempts at making this joint by hand can be seen on small decorative boxes. The glued mitres were cut into with a thin backsaw, then strips of veneer were glued into the cuts.

The hand worker, however, required something stronger, even for such small boxes. Fortunately the joint can be mechanised with basic equipment. It is possible to cut the key sockets with the workpieces mounted in a jig and passed over a circular saw.

There is, however, a definite limit to the size of work that can be safely lifted and stood on its corner on the circular saw bed. A more favoured method is to use a router which enables the jig to be brought to the carcass, however wide it is.

"A more favoured method is to use a router which enables the jig to be brought to the carcass however wide it is"

Completed joint

First, cut the mitres on the 45° router shooting board

Forming the 45° clamping strips using a sawbench cradle

Cramping strips glued on and mitre joint glued together

Cramping strips cleaved and planed off

"If the gluing of a cramping strip should fail, it is better that this should happen now than when the glue is hardening"

Mitres

Begin by cutting the mitres, using a router shooting board at 45°, page 21 for further information.

With the components produced accurately to width and thickness, saw to a shade oversize, say 3mm (⅛in), making sure that these ends are truly square.

Now mark the inside length with a cutting gauge set to thickness plus 1.5mm (1⁄16in).

Cramp the workpiece to the shooting board. Rout to remove the waste down to the line – this is the purpose of marking the inside length.

To make cleaning off glue easier, in many cases it is preferable to polish the insides of the workpiece at this stage.

To assemble wide mitres, 45° cramping strips are required. The jig described, *see below*, will come in handy for other tasks too.

Sawbench cradle

This is made from well-seasoned hardwood. Prepare the two cradle strips accurately to 41 by 41mm (1⅝ by 1⅝in), at least 50mm (2in) longer than the sawbench – if preferred they can be even longer.

Gauge 8mm (5⁄16in) along two faces, then saw and plane away the waste.

Now prepare two 178 by 22 by 22mm (7 by ⅞ by ⅞in) locating strips. Screw these to one of the cradle strips, so that it is a snug fit

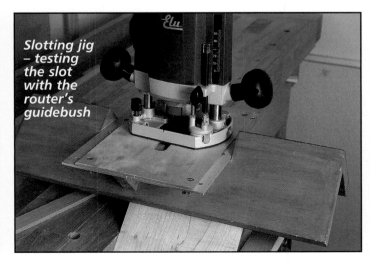
Slotting jig – testing the slot with the router's guidebush

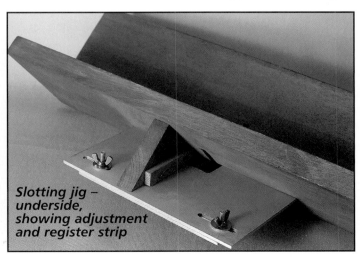
Slotting jig – underside, showing adjustment and register strip

Testing the register strip in the first socket

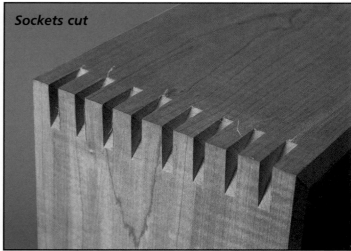

Sockets cut

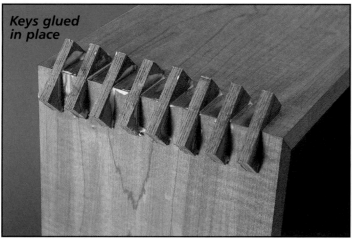

Keys glued in place

Final cleaning up of the joint

on the saw table and parallel to the sawblade.

Then screw on the second strip to complete the cradle.

The slot between the two is accurately arranged by slipping between them at each end a spacer made from offcuts of 5mm (³⁄₁₆in) plywood.

Remove the spacers and, if all is satisfactory so far, dismantle, glue and rescrew. A small cramping block is glued at each end.

Saw off sufficient softwood – chosen for ease of cleaving and planing – to make the cramping strips. The cross-section depends on the size and thickness of the job.

Glue on the cramping strips. The use of Scotch glue allows a rubbed joint to be made. Cramp if preferred.

Assembly

I find that the best assembly method, when making a box for a drawer, is to glue up as two pairs. These can comfortably be stood on edge while the cramps are applied. This method also means that not so many cramps are needed.

The complete construction can then be assembled for a test cramping which will show up any faults.

Also, if the gluing of a cramping strip should fail, it is better that this should happen now than when the glue is hardening. If all is well, the glue can now be applied.

Check for wind – twist – and for equal diagonals. This two-stage method makes fitting a back, bottom or drawer framework easier. Allow 24 hours before splitting off the cramping strips and planing clean.

To show how strong the joint is, a 12.72kg (28lb) weight is placed on the end of the workpiece

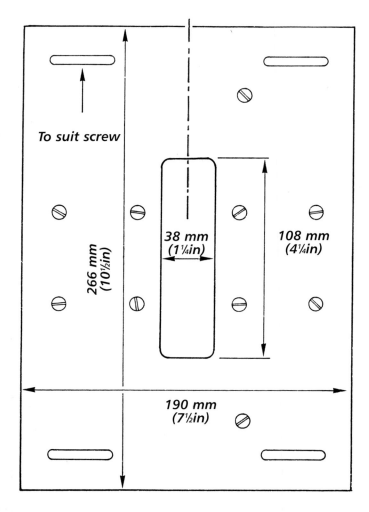

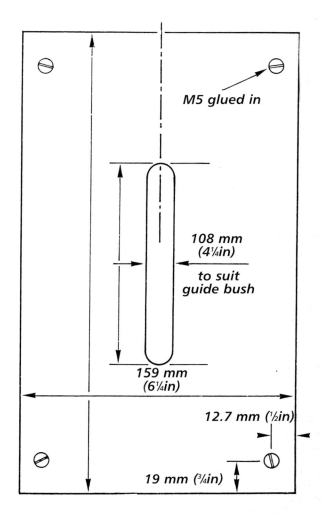

Socketing jig

The construction of the tool for making the key sockets presents no particular difficulties, and the dimensions depend upon the size of the anticipated projects.

Begin by making the gable unit. To prevent any warping, build it from well-seasoned hardwood, best quality plywood or MDF, 19mm (¾in) thick.

Glue up and use either dowels or biscuit joints and a few screws as well, checking that there is an accurate angle of 90° between the inside faces.

Gauge and square the central cut-out. An overhead router does this perfectly but take care not to cut right through.

Two tables are now needed, preferably made from 3mm (⅛in) aluminium sheet or 6mm (¼in) birch plywood.

Make the fixed table according to the drawing. Cut out the central hole and slots, then drill and well-countersink the screw holes.

Screw and, if using ply, also glue, into place.

The moving table is slightly smaller, with screw holes matching the slots on the fixed table.

The central slot is made to take the router's guidebush, and must provide a smooth, sliding fit with no binding and no stop.

M5 countersunk machine screws are held in well-countersunk holes, with a touch of Araldite or Superglue applied to prevent rotation.

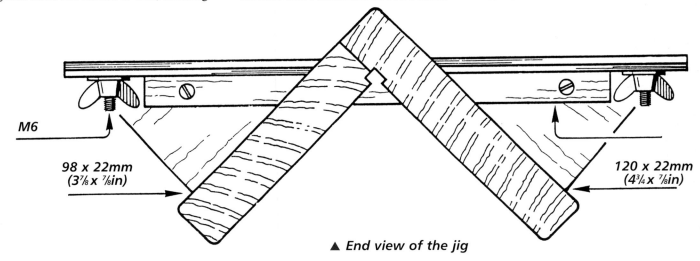

▲ End view of the jig

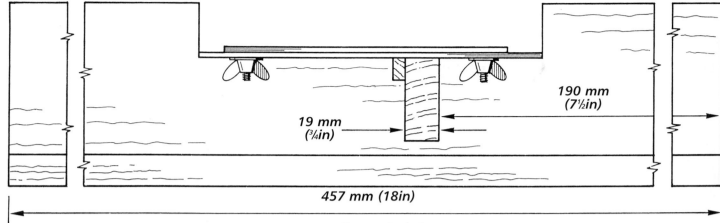

19 mm
(¾in)

190 mm
(7½in)

457 mm (18in)

Suggested sizes

Using the M5 screws, washers and wing-nuts, cramp the moving table to the fixed table so that it is positioned at the extreme right-hand side of the fixed table when viewed from the operator's position.

Fit a ¼in TCT cutter in the router and make a cut through the gable.

With some 13 by 6mm (½ or ¼in) hardwood make a locating strip which is a comfortable sliding fit in this socket; brass, aluminium or bright steel strip would be a more hardwearing option.

Glue and screw two triangular fillets to the gable in such a position that the register strip, in its socket, can be screwed to it. The fillets can be made from offcuts from the gable.

Do not glue the register strip. You may want to change this if other sizes of cutter are used later.

Decide on the spacing required between the keys, and adjust the sliding table to achieve this.

"Move the jig with the router to place the register strip into the socket cut"

Cutting key sockets

Support the job at 45°, either by using the bench vice for small pieces or by sash-cramping to the bench. If much of this jointing is planned, a saddle can be built on which the workpiece is rested; it is automatically set to 45°.

With the register strip hard against one edge, position the jig on the job. If working on a large project, you may want to cramp for this first cut.

Adjust the depth of cut suitably so as not to go through; in fact, leave a good space since excessively long keys are unattractive.

Make the first pass with the router. Do not make a return cut, and do not move the router until all rotation has stopped.

A foot-switch is convenient for this stop-start type of routing.

Move the jig with the router to place the register strip into the socket cut. Make another cut and continue with repeat cuts.

Different cutters produce different socket widths.

Cutting keys

The keys are best produced by thicknesser. If your machine cannot cope with such thin material, lay a piece of

16mm melamine-faced chipboard on the rising table.

Screw a block to one end to prevent it from being fed through the machine. Do not make the keys too tight as they may swell when wet with glue, and refuse to drive home.

Do not try to economise by cutting small triangles since the points will break off when being tapped into place.

Try for thickness in a test cut, and also saw off a piece to make the register strip.

Cut all the keys from the same strip; an odd key which colours differently when polished is quite an eyesore.

For comb jointing, the width of the components must be a multiple of the cutter width, but with the keyed mitre any width can be used.

To avoid endless and tedious adjusting, however, cut half the sockets from one edge and half from the other to form a pleasing arrangement of two groups with an obvious gap at the centre.

After a number of operations, the cradle slot may become larger. Should this happen, glue in two blocks, trim off and rout again. A good fit here reduces spelching – bursting out at the end of the cut.

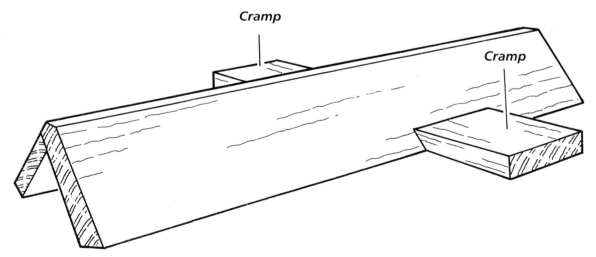

Cramp

Cramp

▲ *Saddle jig for setting the workpiece to an angle of 45°*

Cleaning up after gluing

More work for the versatile routing bars, this time using them when trimming keys and through dovetails

THIS application of my versatile set of routing bars will prove most useful to those of you who have produced the incredibly strong keyed mitre joint featured on page 34.

The excess length of the keys can be taken off with a hand plane, but why not give your router some more work by making a jig to do the job, and one that will also complete a number of other tasks.

The router can take the tedium out of trimming joint keys and through dovetails when combined with this levelling-leg jig; the close accuracy of the finished job can be produced in just a moment.

Much of the key material protruding from the glued joint can be sawn off, when the adhesive is thoroughly set, although caution demands that we don't saw too close, ideally leaving perhaps a skinny 3mm (⅛in).

Hand planing off all that end-grain on say, a set of drawers with eight separate locations each is a boring job, but use of the router does away with all that in a straightforward arrangement that can be applied to any width of joint. This type of joint is often used on the carcassing for decorative cabinets, and when this width of joint has to be cleaned up a mechanised process is a must unless you have plenty of time to spare.

A router set up with a set of routing rods with a levelling leg to remove precisely protruding pins from a drawer joint

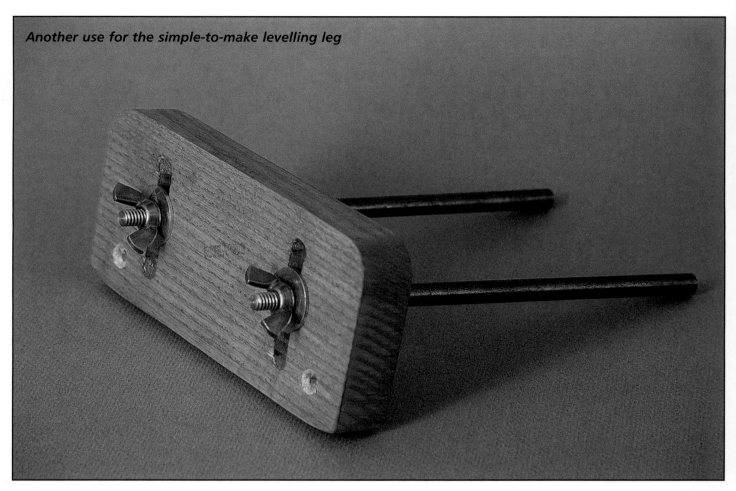

The jig

All that is required for the jig is a set of my routing bars with the adjustable levelling foot attached, see page 10. It is incredibly simple to make and will prove to be useful for many routing tasks.

The rods are fitted to the router and the foot set to a predetermined depth. A good way of doing this is to use a spacer of the required thickness, *see fig 1* – a piece of good quality ¼in birch plywood is perfect.

Sit the baseplate of the router on the

"The router can take the tedium out of trimming joint keys and through dovetails when combined with the levelling leg jig"

spacer, drop the leg to the flat surface below it and tighten the nuts. The spacer is then used to set the levelling block that will support the router on the other side.

To fix the levelling block in place, lay the

joint on a truly flat surface, then position the spacer under it.

Cramp the workpiece and the levelling block together with another piece of the same thickness plywood to the vertical face, sandwiched between them, *see fig 2*.

This extra piece of plywood is used to space the levelling block away from the workpiece so the router cutter runs clear of the block. This avoids the problem of the cutter fouling it and causing it to run off line.

Now up-end the whole lot and fix securely in the vice or on the benchtop.

The router with levelling legs attached is now placed on top of the job and the straight cutter plunged to depth. This must be set precisely and the following method will help to eliminate any fine adjusting and finishing problems.

Setting the levelling block to the correct position and clamping in place

"The paper strip method avoids the cutter causing any damage to the workpiece's surface"

Paper strip method

Set the router on the job, plunge the cutter onto a slip of stout paper, and lock the depth securely. This paper strip method avoids the cutter causing any damage to the workpiece's surface. This could occur if the whole job of cleaning off the pins is done by the router. Fluctuations in the flatness of the surface of the workpiece, no matter how small, will cause the cutter to create small scallops in the surface, meaning that the whole job will need sanding to remove them.

All the waste can now be routed away and, to avoid breakout, cut on each key or dovetail inwards from the corner, feeding INTO the rotation of the cutter.

Once a comfortable rhythm is perfected, the removal of the protruding pins is fast, efficient and accurate.

With the cutter set so the cut is slightly proud of the surface, the minute upstand of the pins remaining can be removed quickly with a single pass of a sharp smoothing plane, followed by sanding and polishing.

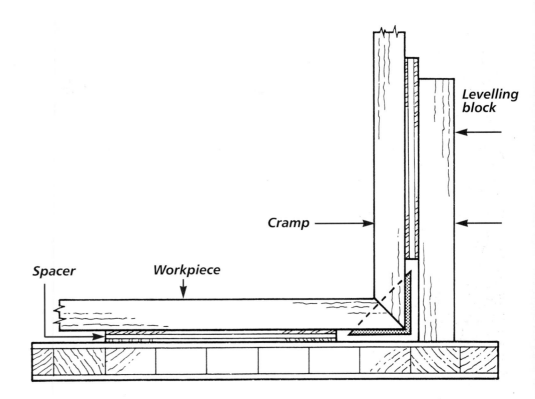

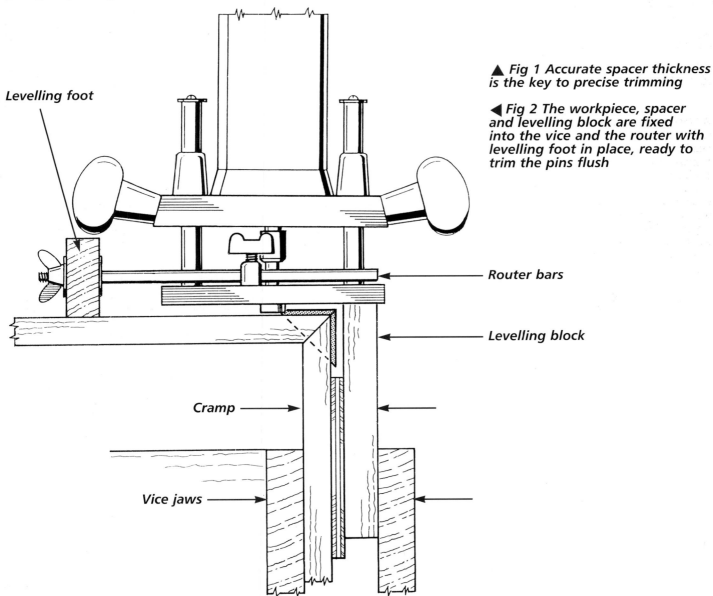

▲ Fig 1 Accurate spacer thickness is the key to precise trimming

◄ Fig 2 The workpiece, spacer and levelling block are fixed into the vice and the router with levelling foot in place, ready to trim the pins flush

How to make strong comb joints

THE comb joint is an alternative to the dovetail, and is surely just as strong. It can be used for any box or carcass project, from small trinket and jewellery boxes to large cabinets.

With an applied front, drawers can also be made like this. Remember that the width of any jointed component must be a multiple of the cutter size.

The construction of the jig is quite straightforward, and should present no difficulty, *see diagrams*. Make it from multi-ply or MDF, as wood may warp.

The model shown was made from oak, but this was very old and very dry, so it has caused me no problems. Although the tables can be made from best quality 6mm (¼in) beech plywood, it is better to use 3mm (⅛in) aluminium alloy sheet.

Drilling, hacksawing and filing are the only metalworking skills needed. To accommodate a differing thickness of workpiece, one jaw is fixed and the other is moveable.

The comb joint is attractive and easy to achieve

Comb joints by router

A simple to make comb-jointing jig helps a router to be even more creative

▶ *The underside of the comb-jointing jig clearly showing the fixed and moving tables*

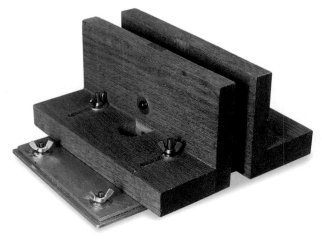

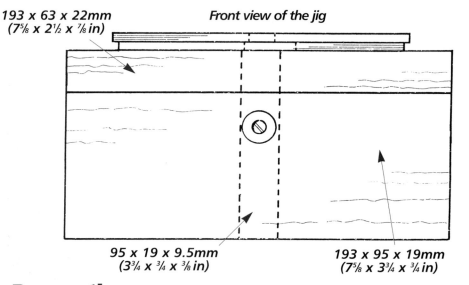

193 x 63 x 22mm
(7⅝ x 2½ x ⅞ in)

Front view of the jig

95 x 19 x 9.5mm
(3¾ x ¾ x ⅜ in)

193 x 95 x 19mm
(7⅝ x 3¾ x ¾ in)

Making table

Now make the moving table. Drill and countersink to match the adjusting slots in the fixed table, then carefully work the central slot. This must be a perfect fit for the router's guidebush.

Keep trying this until you get a smooth, wobble-free motion. Fit the four clamping screws, again with a dab of glue beneath the head, and assemble with wing-nuts and washers.

Jig set-up

Fit the router with a straight cutter of the chosen size and a suitable guidebush. The most commonly used cutter is ¼in.

Close the jaws onto a piece of scrap wood. Set the moving table with its slot near the left hand limit – as seen from the operating position – and clamp.

Preparation

The jaws are almost identical, and the sizes suggested are by no means vital. The moving jaw is slotted, with a cut-out to help remove the chips.

Glue the two components together, checking for a 90° angle between them, and skim over the joints. On the router table, work the two channels which will take the expendable thrust blocks.

Make the thrust blocks a tight but sliding fit. They are secured by round-headed screws and washers.

Suggested sizes are given for the tables. I advise making the fixed one first. The cavity can be any size. Work the four adjusting slots, making an easy fit for the chosen screws.

Secure to the fixed jaw with countersunk wood-screws, and to the moving jaw with machine screws, washers and wing-nuts. For machine screws, 5mm or 3/16in are convenient sizes, while 6mm or ¼in are rather large. Countersink well, and prevent the screws from rotating by applying a touch of epoxy resin glue under the head.

Plan view of tables

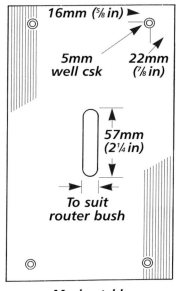

16mm (⅝ in)
5mm
well csk
22mm
(⅞ in)
57mm
(2¼ in)
To suit router bush

Moving table

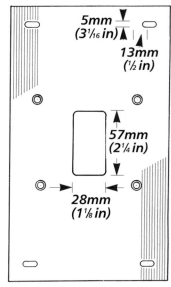

5mm
(3/16 in)
13mm
(½ in)
57mm
(2¼ in)
28mm
(1⅛ in)

Fixed table

Plan view with tables removed

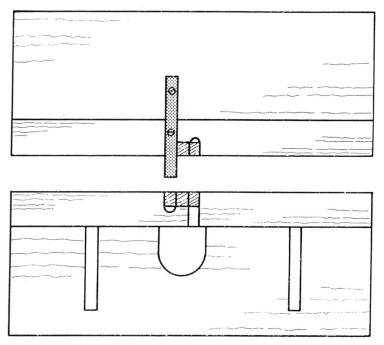

Position the router with the guide bush in the slot. Plunge and lock the cutter to just less than the job thickness, and take a cut into both jaws.

Cut a strip of hardwood to be a snug fit in the slot. Saw off a small piece and screw it in as a locating peg. You may find a piece of square-section metal which matches the cutter size. This is more permanent.

Move the table to the right by the thickness of the cutter. Use as a gauge the off-cut from making the peg.

Grip a piece of scrap wood in the vice. Slip the jig onto it, push firmly up to the locating peg, and cramp there. Take a cut with the router.

"Examine how the two pieces mesh, and adjust until you get a tight fit"

▲ *The workpiece is clamped tightly into a vice and the jig locates in position*

"The cutting will always proceed from the true edge"

▼ *End view showing all clamping devices and locating pin*

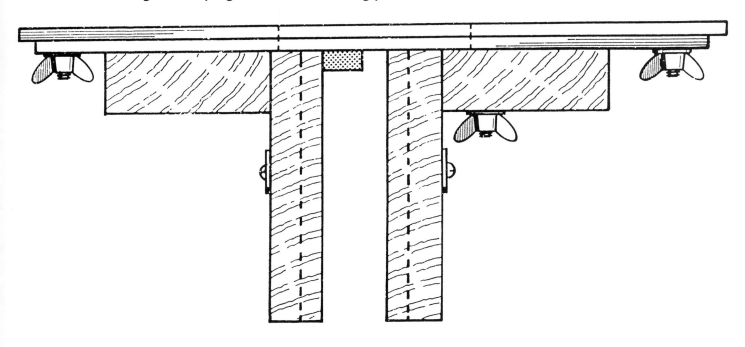

▲ A router with a guidebush fitted is placed on top of the jig to cut all the pins

▲ Once the joint is cut it should be a good fit but not too tight - a light tap with a hammer and protective block is all that should be required

▶ Front view with router in place

Move the jig so the locating peg engages in the socket just produced, and cut again. Continue in this manner across the width of the material, which should be at least as wide as the job.

Repeat on a second piece. Examine how the two pieces mesh, and adjust accordingly until you get a good fit.

Too tight a fit will expel most of the glue, causing glue starvation. The process can be quite time-consuming, so once set up, don't re-adjust. Use the same cutter for subsequent jobs unless a complete change is required.

As with dovetailing, two techniques are available for the length of the pins, so choose your favourite.

Method 1. Adjust the depth of cut to a hairsbreadth over the thickness of the workpiece. Plane the excess after gluing up.

Method 2. Adjust the depth of cut to be a hairsbreadth under the thickness of the workpiece. The whole component is skimmed down to the tops of the teeth.

The first method is easier to clean up; the second is easier to cramp together.

Sockets

Cut the sockets as described, on two identical sides of the box or carcass. On the other two sides, fit the locating peg into the first of the sockets just cut, and bring one of the uncut sides up to it, *see diagram*. Cramp and take a cut.

You now have an open-sided socket. With this against the locating peg, take another cut to produce a complete socket, and continue as before.

It is essential that the true faces and edges are clearly marked. True faces will be on the inside. The cutting will always proceed from the true edge.

When working on grooves or rebates, run through a socket on two components, stopping the router short on the other two to avoid disfiguring the joint.

The normal processes of inside polishing, gluing up, cleaning up, sanding and outside polishing follow.

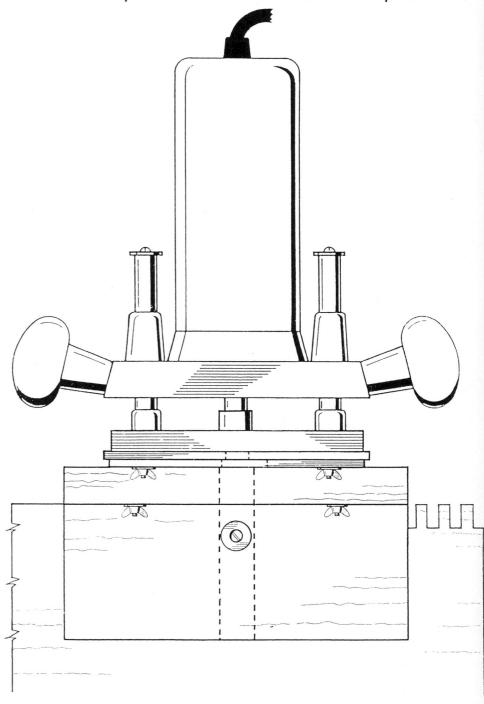

A line of holes

The best technique for drilling holes in a line

OFTEN you'll need a line of holes, such as for adjustable shelf studs, and these can be made easily on a drilling machine or an electric drill in a stand, if you have one.

Gauge the line with a marking or pencil gauge, and step off the centres with dividers. The only aid needed is a board with a fence on it attached to the drill table.

This method works well, but is not so convenient when long parts, such as bookcase sides, are supported on a 255 or 305mm (10 or 12in) drilling table. Once again the router comes to the rescue.

Long parts

You'll need a simple router aid for this job, but not a fully adjustable tool, as it won't be used that often. Make a base from 12mm (½in) multi-ply, it can be slightly larger than the router's base.

To create a row of ¼in holes, fit a straight ¼in cutter, and screw the new base to the router. I chose to use my small Bosch router as it already has convenient holes in the base, although a jig can be made to fit any router.

I used threaded M6. 20mm roofing bolts, easily obtainable, and they suit the purpose admirably.

Countersink the heads of the mounting bolts so they are well below the surface. On some routers it may be necessary to drill two holes in the base and use wood screws.

Distance

Stand the router on some waste, plunge it to drill a ¼in through-hole, and remove the wood base from the router.

Gauge a centre line through this hole and mark on the spacing between the holes the same distance that is required for the shelf spacings. Drill a second ¼in hole on this centre and glue in a short dowel which will be used to locate the jig to create exact spacings between shelf support holes. Make sure the cutter, drill and dowel are all either imperial or metric.

Plug the centre hole, and on its centre drill a large clearance hole, say 32 or 38mm (1½ or 1¼in). Return the base to the router.

Routing a line of holes for shelf support studs is made easy with a router and jig, operator removed for clarity

Decide on the distance of the shelf support holes from the edge of the workpiece, and prepare a spacer strip of this width, minus half of the cutter size, in the case of a ¼in cutter this will be ⅛in.

Prepare a slotted fence from 12mm (½in) ply and screw this to the base using largish repair washers.

To set the fence, let the cutter protrude, and lay the spacer strip against the cutter and the peg. Close up the fence and lock in place, setting the router's depth stop.

"Make sure the cutter, drill and dowel are all either imperial or metric"

Operating

To drill a row of holes, mark the centre of the first hole and drill it to depth, making sure the workpiece is clamped firmly to the benchtop.

Set the peg into this hole and plunge the router. Move the peg to the next hole, plunge and continue in a leapfrog pattern.

Sometimes, for example, building a

▲ *View of the hole drilling jig from underneath*

bookcase with adjustable shelves, you need left and right-hand rows of holes. To get maximum precision, re-set the fence to the other side of the cutter.

Mark the centre of the first hole by squaring across from the original first hole

on the other side – or do this before starting. Drill this separately, as described, and starting with this hole, continue as before.

Using this technique you can arrange a number of different spacings before a new base is needed.

DIMENSIONS OF THE HOLE DRILLING JIG

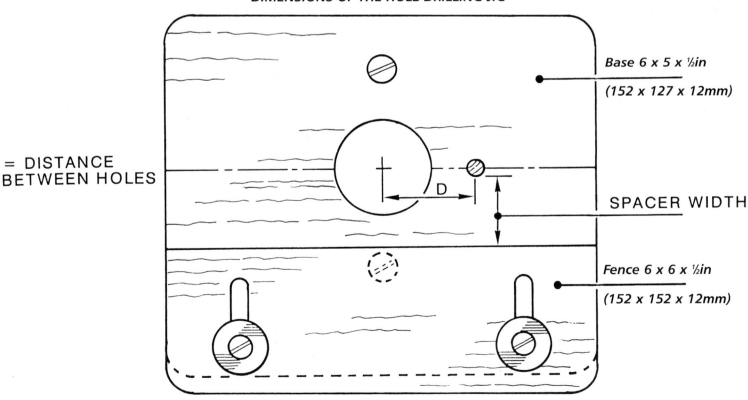

= DISTANCE BETWEEN HOLES

D

Base 6 x 5 x ½in

(152 x 127 x 12mm)

SPACER WIDTH

Fence 6 x 6 x ½in

(152 x 152 x 12mm)

TO FIT BOSCH POF500, ADJUST SIZES TO SUIT

A parking block for the router

Save your blades with a neat little 'parking block'

WE all know that cutters are costly, so we take care of them before and after they rip their way through great chunks of wood – but what about when the cutters are in use?

Picture this scene: the router is set up for a job, the cutter protrudes the correct amount, a number of cuts are to be made, and as you put the router down to change cuts it wobbles over and the blade snaps.

So, where do you park the router safely between cuts, so the cutter won't snap? The answer lies in a hand-made 'parking block'. Once made, the parking block can be kept handy on the benchtop while working, and will protect your hardware evermore.

You can use any suitably sized offcuts, mine was made from three layers of 12mm multi-ply, glued together.

Having glued-up, tidy the edges to a convenient shape, rounding the corners on the disc sander. Centrally, drill a 25mm (1in) hole right through the block.

That's it. The blade will sit protected inside the hole without damaging the benchtop, and no chance of it wobbling over.

Why didn't I think of this 30 years ago?

▲ **Convenient parking for a router with a protruding cutter**

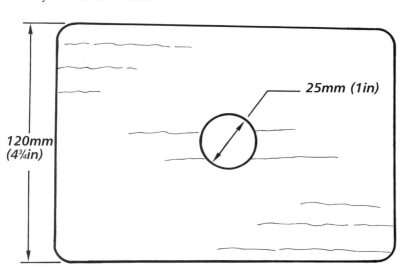

25mm (1in)

120mm (4¾in)

36mm (1⁷⁄₁₆in)

170mm (6¾in)

Dimensions of a parking block

"So, where do you park the router safely between cuts, so the cutter won't snap?"

Loose tooth comb joint

Make your own version of this simple but versatile loose tooth comb joint

HERE is a comb joint variation which is both strong and decorative, but without the very precise setting-up process of the standard comb joint, see page 43.

Also, the width of the workpiece need not be a multiple of the tooth size, and the joint can be made with this quickly improvised jig, as well as the comb jointing tool (above).

The jig

Glue and screw together two pieces of 19mm (¾in) multi-ply, blockboard or MDF, to form the right-angle jig for creating the routed sockets of this joint. Next, produce a wood or metal strip to suit the mitre-slide groove in your router table, and screw it in place on the underside of the jig. Its position and size will depend on your set-up.

Glue a strengthening block centrally over the expected position of the cut, and fit a knob or handle to make operating the jig easier.

Make a movable face that will set the spacings of the sockets, from 9mm (⅜in) plywood. It should be about the same size as the working face of the jig with holes drilled for its bolts.

Cramp it in place on the jig and mark through the holes for the position of the slots in the jig. Then, using a side fence on your router, and a small straight cutter, cut the slots about 38mm (1½in) long to give the face the movement it will require.

Finally, set up the router in the router table and fit a cutter the right size for the teeth.

Making the joint

Set the cutter height a fraction greater than the workpiece thickness, then take a cut into the jig until there is a slot routed well into the jig. Next, remove the movable face. Then thickness a strip of hardwood and glue a short piece of it into the moveable face's slot as a location peg.

Attach the face back onto the working face of the jig, and slide it offset from the cutter to give the desired spacing between the sockets.

The loose tooth comb joint is quick and versatile

▲ This simple jig is made up of two pieces of ply-wood fixed together at right-angles

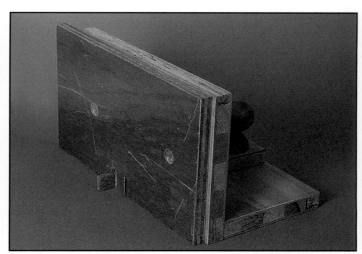

▲ The front of the jig shows the moveable face with its locating peg

Unlike a conventional comb joint jig, you don't need to have equally spaced teeth and sockets with this joint, and in the specimen joint shown I have deliberately exaggerated them.

This is a matter of taste, so if you are not confident about creating an unusual joint, attempt to make them even. If they are unequally spaced all the matching sockets will have to be machined on the same off-set setting.

A quick way of getting even spacings is to cut half of the sockets from one edge, and half from the other. This gives two groups of teeth with a central gap that, although it may not be the same as the other socket spacings, which can be quite an attractive feature, it is easy to make adjustments to make them all even.

In the joint shown I just struck lucky with my choice of settings, so the central gap is indistinguishable.

If you want the first socket nearer to the edge, cramp on a stop block and make the first cut on all the components, remove the block and continue using the locating peg.

Tooth material

Prepare the tooth material using a planer-thicknesser or a router set up as a micro thicknesser. Double-ended router rods can be used for this operation. Generally, a circular saw is often not finely adjustable enough, nor will it give a good enough finish.

The strip should be a tight fit in the sockets, but not too tight, as this will cause glue starvation. The width is just greater than the workpiece thickness.

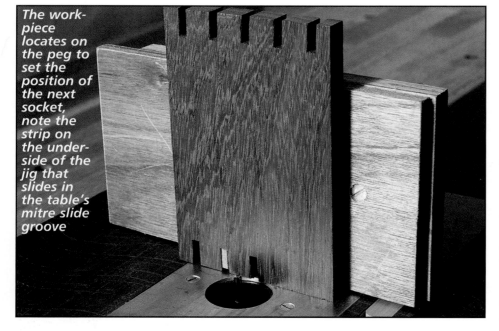

The work-piece locates on the peg to set the position of the next socket, note the strip on the under-side of the jig that slides in the table's mitre slide groove

▼ Thin strips for the pins are machined to thickness using a router and the new router rods

▼ Sockets and pins ready to fit together

▲ *First, glue the pins into one workpiece ...*

▲ *... then plane them flush on both faces*

Saw off to length, just over twice the workpiece thickness. I usually touch up the ends that will be inside the joint on my disc sander for a better fit, and make a few spares.

Mark which components are to have the teeth fitted first, and apply glue to the appropriate sockets.

Most glues will be suitable. I use Titebond, a cold-setting hide glue which gives a long assembly time. Check in advance the glue won't stain the timber.

Tap in the teeth with a light hammer, making sure they bed down thoroughly, and project a little on both sides. Remove any exuded glue with a damp toothbrush and rag, then leave overnight to harden. When dry, skim the teeth level on both sides with a hand plane so they are exactly the same thickness as the component.

Skimming

Now the two parts of the joint can be fitted together. Apply the glue and tap the joint together. As with a dovetail, the joint should tap together, but in practice some light cramping is often needed. Wipe off surplus glue, particularly from the inside corner, and leave overnight to dry.

Skim the joints flush, planing inwards to avoid spelching, using a sharp, finely-set jack plane.

I use a jack plane rather than a smoother because there is a good length of sole in front of the cutter to get settled on the work before the cut begins.

Although I chose to remove the waste by hand, I showed you my method for doing the same job with a router.

Gently tap the joint together, use a soft block to protect the workpiece

Wipe off excess glue and trim the pins flush

Sand and polish

I made the teeth from contrasting wood, beech (Fagus sylvatica) into makore (Tieghemella heckelii), to get a clearer photograph. You can use contrasting woods in a job, but beware of making the piece look too garish.

Also, make sure all the teeth come from the same strip, or when polished the teeth may be of different colours, spoiling the decorative effect.

This is a quick way of making a number of identical sturdy storage containers, tool drawers and the like. The joint is equally effective in joining two components of different thicknesses.

A mini combination

How to handle the fiddly bits with a miniature combination machine

MACHINING a good finish on extremely thin pieces of wood is a problem that isn't easily solved by many machines that you will find in the workshop. Pushing thin components of say, ¼in or less, through a thicknesser is hazardous to the material as it will tend to disintegrate. The circular saw can't be relied upon to produce well-finished thin strips.

Yet small section stock is in constant demand by musical instrument makers, model makers, toy makers, doll's house furnishers and of course cabinetmakers engaged in fine detail work.

The solution is a tool you already have – your router!

Mini machine

My miniature combination machine is a jig that solves all these problems, and at a reasonable price. It has three requirements. First, the router.

I assume you have one, otherwise why would you be reading this book? Even the most modest router will do. Secondly, some pieces of plywood to make the wooden base, *see photo 1*, which is straightforward to produce. Finally, a pair of new double-ended Vanguard Router Rods, either 8mm or 10mm.

The woodwork

The sizes of the jig shown suit the Bosch POF and the Elu 96 routers, but if needed just modify them to suit the router and the Router Rods you use.

Make the jig from either best quality birch multi-ply, MDF, or old well-seasoned hardwood.

Cut the the baseboard to size, *see fig A*, then screw on a central block for gripping the jig in a vice, *see fig B*.

Next, make the two bearers for the Router Rods. Cut them to size and produce, either by routing or by drilling and sawing, vertical slots, *see photo 2*, at the correct spacing apart for the holes in your router's baseplate so the router can be set to different heights. For 6mm rods make these ¼in to give an easy sliding fit.

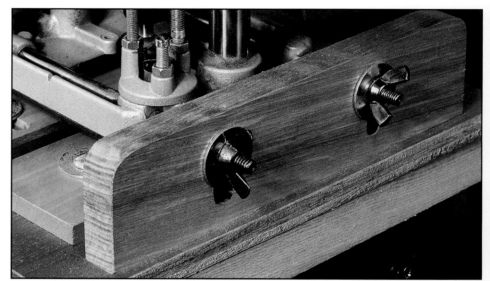

▲ *Photo 2 Slots in the bearers allow the router's height to be set*

Screw, from the underside, and glue the first bearer in place onto the baseboard, its exact position isn't critical but make sure it is parallel to the edge of the baseboard.

▼ *Photo 3 Thickness with the workpiece held by the fences*

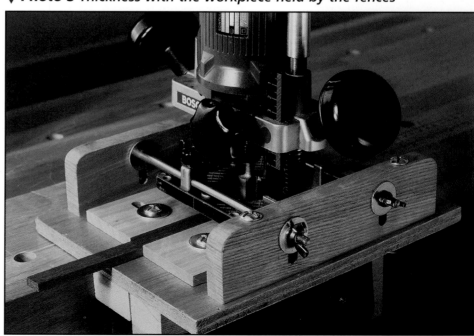

machine

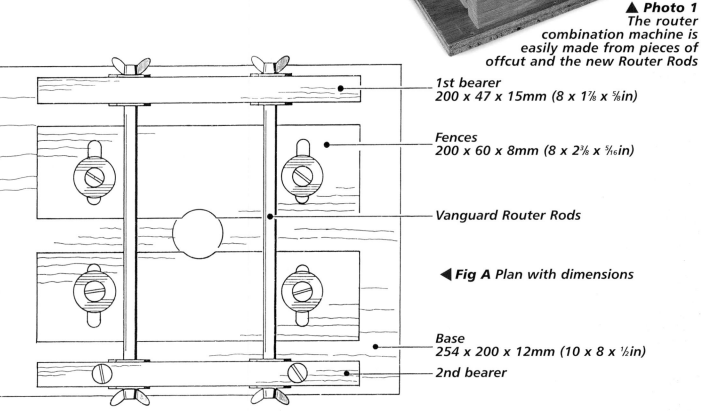

1st bearer
200 x 47 x 15mm (8 x 1⅞ x ⅝in)

Fences
200 x 60 x 8mm (8 x 2⅜ x ⁵⁄₁₆in)

Vanguard Router Rods

◀ **Fig A** Plan with dimensions

Base
254 x 200 x 12mm (10 x 8 x ½in)

2nd bearer

The second bearer is drilled through with ¼in holes to take M6 roofing bolts, *see fig C*, which holds it to the baseboard, but can be removed to allow the fitting of a router. Assemble the pieces together, on the baseboard, with the bars and washers in place. Place a thin card washer under the inside washers to make sure there is some room for movement when re-assembled. Mark the baseboard, through the holes in the bearer, with the ¼in wood drill.

Dismantle and drill through the base-board with about a ⅟₁₆in drill. Fit two M6 T-nuts to the underside – available from decent hardware shops. Carefully drill a shallow cavity for their flange at ¾in, then follow through with a ⁵⁄₁₆in or 8mm wood drill. Do not hammer these in. Instead, draw them in gently with an M6 bolt, washer and wood block, *see fig D*.

Now assemble the bearer back onto the baseboard and check, without the card washers, that the rods ride easily up and down in the bearers' slots. If tight, enlarge the slots slightly.

▼ **Fig B** Side view

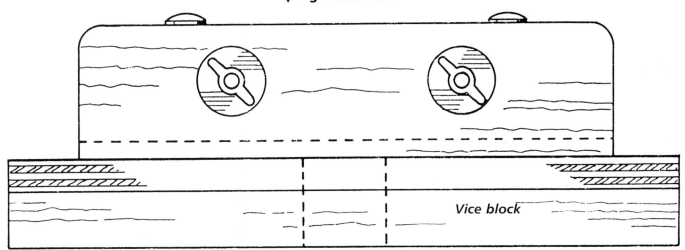

Vice block

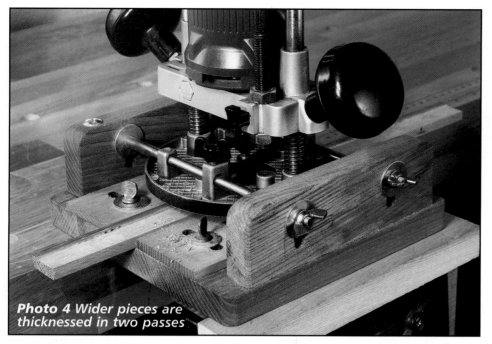

Photo 4 *Wider pieces are thicknessed in two passes*

Photo 5 *Two cuts may be needed for deep rebates*

"In time the fences will be cut into by various cutters"

Setting up

Remove the second bearer and the Router Rods. Slide these into the router, assemble them back onto the jig then slide the router to the centre of the jig and lock in place.

Make a setting-up block from ¾in multi-ply and possibly a second from ½in ply. Slide this under the router's baseplate and on top of the baseboard, slacken the wing-nuts and drop the router onto the block. Tighten all the wing-nuts on the Router Rods, which will hold the router perfectly parallel to the baseboard, then slide out the block.

Plunge the router, fitted with any size of straight cutter, to cut the faintest mark in the baseboard. Drill a 25mm (1in) diameter through-hole centred on this mark which will allow the use of cutters with a nut on their end.

Prepare two fences and suitably slot them. Chamfer a small dust-groove on their underside and add identifying marks for re-positioning. Hold them in place and draw through the slots onto the base.

Mark the centres of these slots for the locking screws, then drill through the baseboard and fit M6 T-nuts as already described, *see fig D*. Remember to position the holes clear of the router base so they don't interfere with the screwdriver.

Secure the fences with short M6 roofing bolts and repair washers. In time the fences will be cut into by various cutters, but this doesn't matter.

The jig is now complete and machining can begin.

▼ **Fig C** *End view*

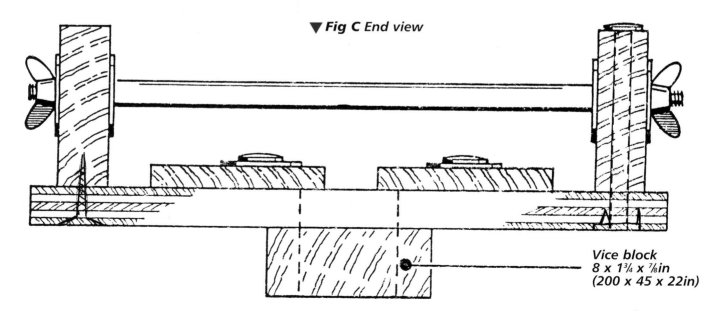

Vice block
8 x 1¾ x ⅞in
(200 x 45 x 22in)

Photo 6 A constant feed speed is required to stop mouldings burning

"This process will show up any sloppy work in making the jig"

Thicknessing wider pieces

Components can be thicknessed that are almost twice the cutter size, such as 1⅛ in when using a 1in cutter. Set the fences so the cut will just pass the centre line, *see photo 4*.

Take a cut here, then reverse the wood end-for-end and feed in again. This process will show up any sloppy work in making the jig, which will result in the joint between the two cuts being visible.

Edging

Quite thin material can be successfully edged or produced to width by the same method as thicknessing. Bring up the fences to support to the workpiece. Naturally, use a cutter considerably wider than the workpiece.

Rebating

The set-up is basically the same as for thicknessing, *see photo 5*. Fit a suitably sized cutter, position the two fences and make any final adjustments by sliding the router along the bars.

I prefer two light cuts to one heavy cut, and for a good finish always end with a fine cut.

When cutting rebates always feed in the work so the cutter is revolving into the workpiece, *see fig E*, otherwise it is liable to be snatched.

Grooving

Set up as described for rebating. Fit the required cutter and adjust for depth, then lock. Make any fine position adjustments across the workpiece by sliding the router along the bars.

Form the groove by making several gentle cuts and keep it pressed down firmly onto the base. Again, if hand holding-down makes you feel uncomfortable make up a couple of hold-down devices.

Thicknessing

Saw the material approximately to thickness and parallel. Fit a large straight cutter, ¾in or if available a 1in.

Insert the workpiece into the jig centrally and plunge the non-running router so the cutter just grips it. Move the two fences to either side of the workpiece, lock them and then release the router.

The fit of the fences on the workpiece must be neither too tight, to allow easy movement, nor too slack, to permit wobble.

The depth of cut is now set. I found two easy ways of setting a fine cut.

If you have a fine depth adjuster fitted, plunge the router so the non-running cutter touches the workpiece, and lock there. Remove the workpiece, adjust the fine depth adjuster to give a cut then lock the depth setting.

The second method is to plunge the non-running cutter onto a workpiece and lock there. Remove the workpiece, then drop the depth stop onto its turret stop with a piece of card or veneer between, and lock that also. Now plunge the router to take up the thickness of the card.

The workpiece can now be fed through, *see photo 3*, and the process repeated until the correct thickness is achieved. Rout all similar components at the same cut and resist the urge to take heavy cuts.

The work must be held down firmly where it goes under the router and then emerges. I find that I can do this by hand but if it makes you feel uncomfortable make up a couple of hold-down devices.

"As with all moulding work, to avoid burning, feed through steadily without stopping"

▼ *Fig D Drawing in a T-nut, do not hammer in*

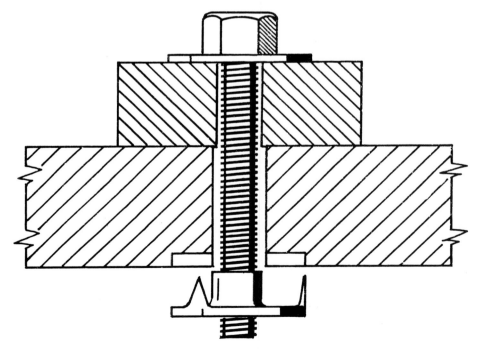

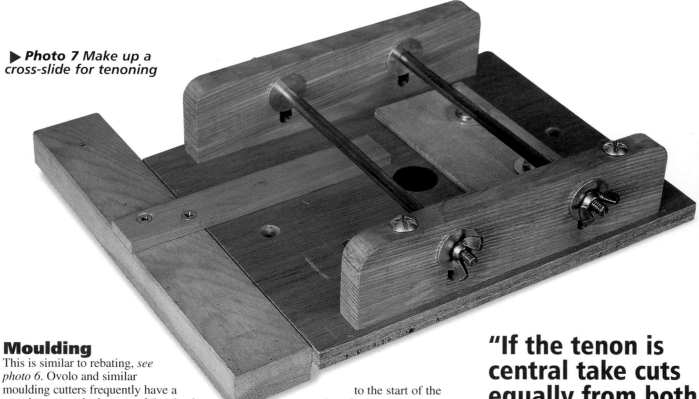

▶ **Photo 7** *Make up a cross-slide for tenoning*

Moulding

This is similar to rebating, *see photo 6.* Ovolo and similar moulding cutters frequently have a securing nut at the bottom of the shank. This is accommodated in the central hole of the jig.

As with rebating, the workpiece must be fed against the direction of cut, mouldings can be worked using only one fence.

If the cutter has a guidebush the fences can be dispensed with but it may be safer to position a fence to keep the workpiece on-line.

As with all moulding work, to avoid burning, feed through steadily without stopping.

Chamfering

This is tackled in the same way as moulding, using a 45° cutter. Position the fences and the router and set a depth stop on the router to give the width of chamfer required.

For stopped chamfers use only one fence. Push the workpiece onto the cutter until it stops at the fence, then move it until it cuts to the start of the chamfer. Feed the work through the jig then pull it away from the fence when the other end of the chamfer is reached.

It is vital to move the workpiece immediately, otherwise it will burn in a visible position which will be hard to hide or remove.

Small mortices

Mortices of say, ¼ and ³⁄₁₆in, can be cut conveniently in small components.

Set the fences up as for edging, fit the appropriate cutter then centralise the router over the mortice position, finally, set the depth stop.

Start by plunging to make a series of touching holes at full depth, take care not to burn with the first cut.

Slide the workpiece through to clear the waste from the mortice then trim the ends square, or round over the ends of the tenons.

"If the tenon is central take cuts equally from both sides"

Small tenons

Providing they are small, tenons can be cut easily and accurately. To avoid break-out at the end of the cut, as often happens when routing end grain, remove the fences and make a simple right-angle jig, *see photo 7.*

If the tenon is central, as it generally is, take cuts equally from both sides. Again, gentle cuts are required and rout by sliding the right-angle jig across the baseboard, *see photo 8.*

Only one tenon needs to be set up on an offcut the same dimensions as the workpiece, testing frequently in the mortice. When satisfied with the fit, set the depth gauge so the joint can be repeated without further effort.

Photo 8 *The workpiece is moved across the jig for tenoning*

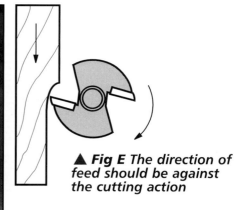

▲ **Fig E** *The direction of feed should be against the cutting action*

Splined mitre joint

How to rout the invisible splined mitre joint

THE corners of cabinets and carcasses where there is no overhang of the top or upstand of the sides present a jointing problem. The strongest solutions are the common or through dovetail, the lap dovetail, the comb joint or the keyed mitre joint. I have recently described how all three work.

Concealed

In the eyes of some workers, these joints, however strong, all suffer from the same defect. The joint is visible. When for a smooth appearance a concealed joint is called for, there are few choices.

There is the double lap dovetail, with a moulding concealing the lap, or the secret mitre dovetail. These are connoisseur's joints, fine for the gifted amateur to show off his skill, but for the small professional, unfortunately, few clients will be prepared to pay for the time and the high skill.

So what to do? Once again it is router to the rescue, in the form of the splined mitre joint. The glued mitre has virtually no strength and is of little use beyond small picture frames. It needs to be strengthened either by inserted keys, which will be visible, see page 21, or by a lengthwise spline.

▲ *The splined mitre joint is strong and simple to create*

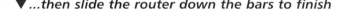

▼*Rout the mitre in two passes if necessary, first the top...*   ▼*...then slide the router down the bars to finish*

▲ Then, rout the slot along the mitre
▼ Cross-section through the mitre cutting operation

"Once again it is router to the rescue, in the form of the splined mitre joint"

Working in the mitre

Prepare the components to width and thickness. Mark the inside length at each end, then saw off square at the outside length, plus ⅟₁₆in at each end. Using the 45° router shooting board, feed in the workpiece with a piece of hardboard underneath.

Lay a piece of flat chipboard or blockboard across the runners, push up the workpiece to it and clamp with the clamp bar.

Set up the router with a ½ or ¾in cutter. Even the most modest router will do. Set the fence to run along the top rail. Adjust the bars then plunge sufficiently to take a cut from the corner. Work from right to left, against the rotation of the cutter. Slowly increase the cut, sliding the router down the bars when it becomes necessary.

Continue in this manner until the marked inside line is reached and the full width of the mitre has been cut. The final adjustment will take the cutter just into the hardboard. Finish with a fast fine cut to give the best finish, and set the depth stop.

"Work from right to left, against the rotation of the cutter"

Working the groove

There are now two options. One is to complete the remaining seven mitres and then change the cutter to cut the grooves. The other is to have a second router set up to

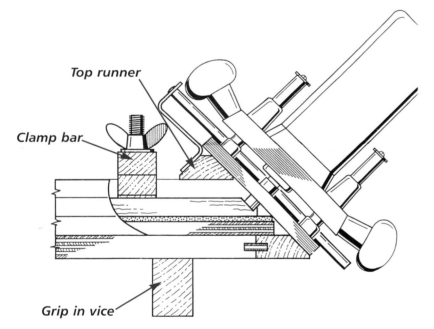

Top runner

Clamp bar

Grip in vice

▼ If the ends of the carcass are seen, stop the slot short of the ends

▼ The splines must be made from plywood that exactly fits the slots, through and stopped versions are shown here

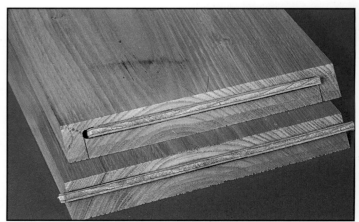

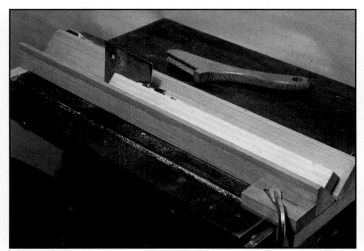

▲ Make up a jig to cut triangular clamping blocks on the saw, crown guard removed for clarity

▲ Glue and clamp the blocks on the centre line of the mitre

▼ Cross-section through the slot cutting operation

complete the joint on this component at one cramping. I use the second method. The procedure will be the same, but it will save time.

A word first on the spline. This will be made from plywood. Long grain solid wood is liable to split, while the preparation of short grain splines is tedious.

'Stoutheart' plywood is ideal. The thick inner layer is in fact short grain, giving the greater strength. The most useful timber for this purpose is 4 to 6mm ply. This means one or two metric cutters may be needed.

North America will use $\frac{3}{16}$ and $\frac{1}{4}$in plywood, which occasionally can still be found here. The point is that the cutter should match the plywood available. Near enough will not do.

Position the cutter over the already cut mitre and locate the cutter. Note that the groove is not cut central, but is worked a little nearer the inside. This gives a deeper groove. Carefully set the depth stop before starting the cut. For the simplest form of the joint the cutter runs right through.

For quality carcass work, stop the groove short at each end by about $\frac{1}{2}$in. For a box construction, where the lid is later sawn off, carefully mark, then stop the groove on each side of the parting line.

Now prepare the plywood splines, about $\frac{1}{16}$in narrower than the combined depth of the two grooves. Sand off any rough edges to give easy entrance. Cut to length, then also cut two 1in pieces for testing the joint, *see below*.

Obviously the joint cannot be effectively cramped as it stands. Resist the temptation to cramp up with picture frame type string or webbing cramps. They are not strong enough. Glued on triangle cramping strips are necessary.

"For a box-like construction, first glue together the diagonally opposite joints"

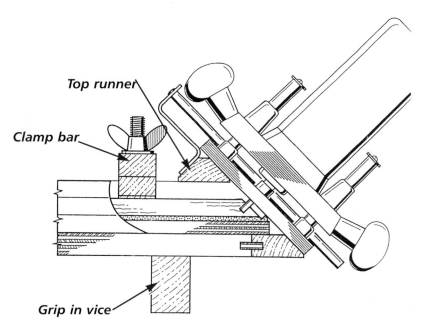

Top runner

Clamp bar

Grip in vice

▼ Plan of saw table jig for cutting the triangular clamping blocks

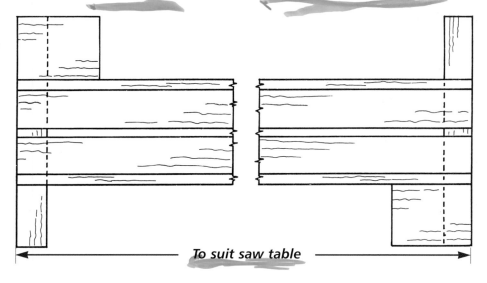

To suit saw table

▲ *Clamp the joint together using the glued-on blocks*

▲ *When dry, plane the softwood blocks off*

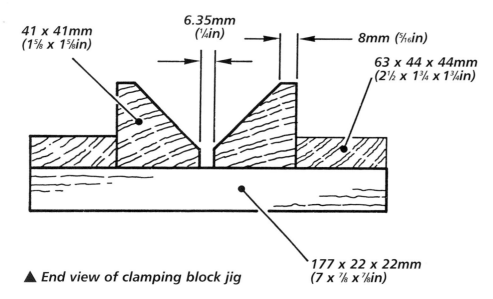

41 x 41mm
(1⅝ x 1⅝in)

6.35mm
(¼in)

8mm (⁵⁄₁₆in)

63 x 44 x 44mm
(2½ x 1¾ x 1¾in)

177 x 22 x 22mm
(7 x ⅞ x ⅞in)

▲ *End view of clamping block jig*

Sawbench cradle

Make the cradle from well-seasoned hardwood. Prepare the two cradle strips very accurately to 1⅝ by 1⅝in, at least two inches longer than the sawbench. If preferred, they can be even longer. Gauge ⁵⁄₁₆in along two faces, then saw and plane away the waste.

Prepare two locating strips; 7 by ⅞ by ⅞in would be about right. Screw these to one of the cradle strips to be a snug fit on the saw table, and parallel to the saw blade. Screw on the second to complete the cradle.

The slot between the two is accurately arranged by sliding a spacer between them at each end. These are offcuts of ⁵⁄₁₆in plywood. Remove the spacers. If all is satisfactory so far, dismantle, glue and re-screw. A small cramping block is glued at each end as shown.

Saw off enough softwood to make the cramping strips. Softwood cleaves and planes off most easily. The cross-section will depend on the size and thickness of the job.

Set up the cradle on the sawbench, return the crown guard and cramp securely. Check the sawblade is central in the slot and not binding or catching. With two pushsticks, feed through the softwood strip, producing the necessary triangular sections. Cut up to the width of the job.

If using the bandsaw the jig will need slight modification. Instead, glue up the cradle on a piece of thin plywood. When dry, feed into the bandsaw until several inches behind the blade. Cramp the bandsaw table and feed in the prepared softwood.

Now glue on the cramping strips. Using scotch glue, a rubbed joint can be made. Cramp if preferred. Scotch glue will later clean off more easily than the glass-hard synthetic resins. Leave to harden overnight.

Finishing off

To test the joint, fit in the two small plywood strips and cramp up with several cramps.

If all is well, clean up and polish the insides, having worked any groove or rebate for top, bottom or back. Take care not to get any wax on the mitre itself. If necessary this can be protected with plastic or masking tape.

Glue up. I use synthetic resin glue, such as Aerolite or Cascamite rather then PVA61, but this is up to you.

For a box-like construction, first glue together the diagonally opposite joints. The job will now stand up while the two remaining joints are glued. Surplus glue will flake off the polished inside surfaces.

Cleave off the cramping strips, (this is why softwood is recommended), then plane flush, scrape, sand and finish.

My tests have shown this to be a very strong joint, and quite adequate for most carcass work.

Router setting gauge

How to make a neat little setting gauge for the router

T HIS is one of those handy little tools which, once made, you wonder how you managed without it. Although the metalwork can be made by anyone with a metalturning lathe, for the price at which it is offered by Vanguard Cutting Tools, it is hardly worth the effort.

The depth setting block can be used to set the depth that a router cutter is set in relation to the router's baseplate, the rod can be pre-set to a measured depth or inverted into say, a groove, and the setting transferred to the cutter, bypassing any measuring.

"It is vital that the block width and the rod length should be exactly the same"

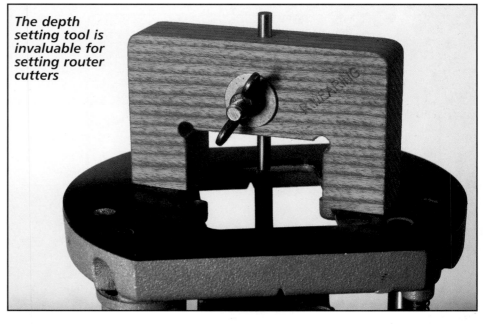

The depth setting tool is invaluable for setting router cutters

A groove's depth can be set and transferred to the cutter without measuring

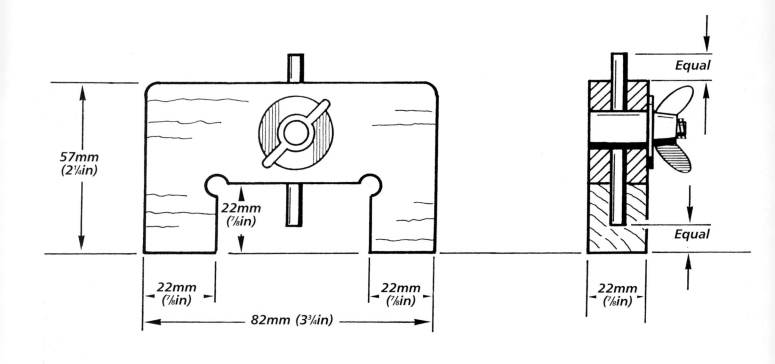

57mm
(2¼in)

22mm
(⅞in)

22mm
(⅞in)

22mm
(⅞in)

82mm (3¾in)

Equal

Equal

22mm
(⅞in)

Front view

Section at centre

▲ *Router setting tool's suggested sizes*

Block

Make the block from any good dense hardwood. The 82 by 57mm (3¼ by 2¼in) sizes shown are only suggestions, but they suit me perfectly. Prepare the rectangular block and mark out the centre lines on the face and top edge.

Do all the drilling, if possible, using a drilling machine or a drill stand to ensure stability and accurately positioned holes.

First bore a ½in hole through the side of the block for the barrel of the draw bolt. This size is chosen because ½in wood boring bits are more common than 12 or 13mm. Next drill a hole vertically down through the block for the depth rod, a ⁷⁄₃₂in or 5.5mm drill bit gives an easy sliding fit for the rod.

To make the cutout in the block I first drilled the corners as shown on the drawing, then removed the waste with the bandsaw. The drilled, round corners eliminate the messy clean-up of a sawn, right-angled inside corner.

Rod length

Note that it is worth initially preparing the block minutely wider than the length of the rod. Then with the metalwork in place, stand the depth tool on a flat surface and drop the rod to touch it. The top of the block can then be brought down flush with the top of the rod. I found that just a touch on my disc sander was all that was needed.

It is vital that the block width and the rod length should be exactly the same. This ensures that the cutter depth setting on the router is the same as the depth gauge setting, the distance from the top of the block to the top of the rod. Thus, if the required depth of the cut is set on the depth gauge, the router setting will be the same, or vice versa.

When satisfied with the tool a coat of oil or sealer will keep it looking smart.

If the depth gauge is intended to measure grooves narrower than 5mm (³⁄₁₆in), file two flats on the end of the rod.

When ordering from Vanguard specify that you want the Router Setting Tool. Vanguard Cutting tools, Sheffield (see Appendix, page 102).

Fielding panels

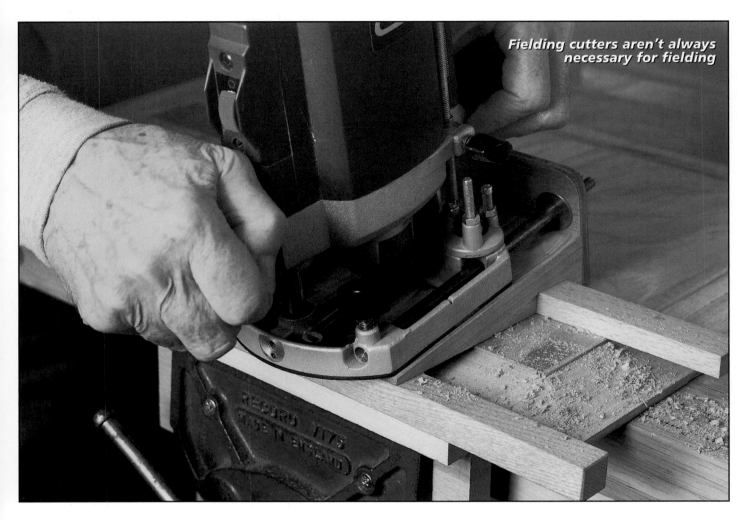

Fielding cutters aren't always necessary for fielding

You don't need fielding cutters to field panels

THE fielding of a number of similar identical panels by hand is quite a time consuming task, and we don't all have that amount of spare time to devote to our woodwork. It is sometimes recommended, particularly in American publications, that panels can be fielded on the circular saw. With a tilted saw or table and the crown guard removed, this is a hazardous operation, certainly not to be encouraged.

Expensive fielding cutters are available for the large heavy-duty routers, but these generally fit only the only the larger collets, so are not applicable to many readers who I classify as 'advanced garage workers'.

"When step-fielding the angle will be found to be slightly under-cut"

Getting started

The method I describe here will suit even the most modest of routers. I have used it with the Bosch POF and the Elu MOF96, and have found the arrangement to be satisfactory for most of my panels.

Draw a section through the panel,

two or three times enlarged to ascertain the required angle of slope. What is needed is not the angle measured in degrees, but the incline, say 1½ inches in 5 inches.

Produce the base block to size, mark the true face, then gauge the thickness at each end. If material thick enough is not available, the block can be built up from three pieces, already angled.

Bore a central hole of 1in, saw and plane the waist, checking that the new face is truly flat. Saw the slot then turn the job over so the true face is on top. Cut a housing in the lower face and fit the stabilising rail.

▼ End view of panel fielding jig

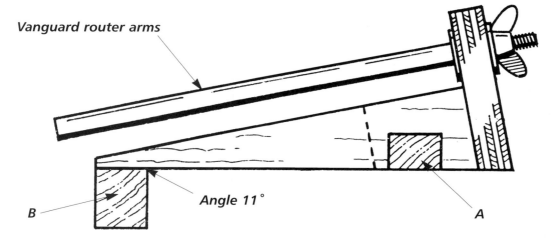

Vanguard router arms

B

Angle 11°

A

This is to steady the tool at the start and end of the cut where there is a liability of the tool to tip. Glue and screw the fence to the thin end.

Now make the plywood piece which takes the router arms. Screw this to the bed block using long woodscrews, as they are going into the end grain.

Clamp a pencil into the bar sockets on the router, most pencils will fit comfortably into 8mm or ⁵⁄₁₆in holes, and scribe the centre heights. Mark the bar centres to this line.

Remove the ply piece and drill the holes oversize to permit slight adjustment if needed. For example, for 6mm threads use 8mm or ⁵⁄₁₆in. Screw back into place.

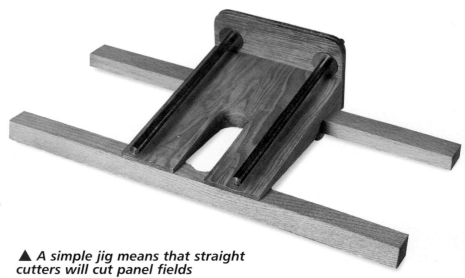

▲ A simple jig means that straight cutters will cut panel fields

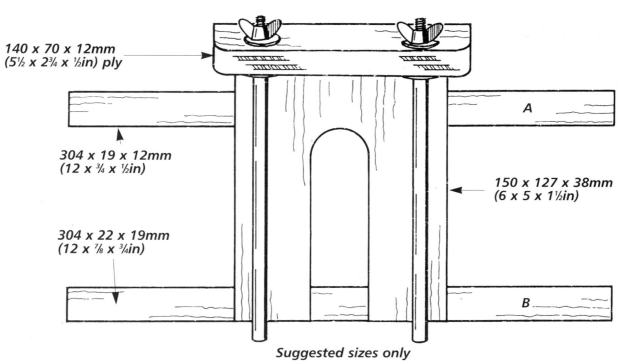

140 x 70 x 12mm (5½ x 2¾ x ½in) ply

304 x 19 x 12mm (12 x ¾ x ½in)

304 x 22 x 19mm (12 x ⅞ x ¾in)

A

150 x 127 x 38mm (6 x 5 x 1½in)

B

Suggested sizes only

▲ Plan view of panel fielding jig

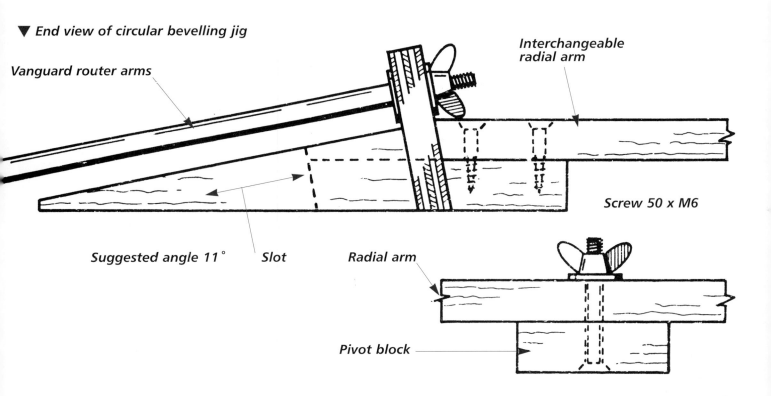

▼ *End view of circular bevelling jig*

Vanguard router arms

Interchangeable radial arm

Screw 50 x M6

Suggested angle 11°　　*Slot*　　*Radial arm*

Pivot block

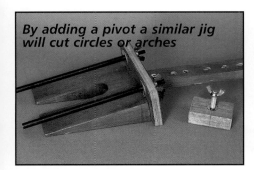

By adding a pivot a similar jig will cut circles or arches

"Most pencils will fit comfortably into 8mm or ⁵⁄₁₆in holes"

Mullet

Fit the router with the largest straight cutter available. For small routers this will be ¾in or possibly 1in. Slide in the router bars then completely assemble the router and the tool. Slacken the router and check that it slides sweetly along the bars.

Plunge, look, and take a cut at the end of the panel. Slide up the bars, increase the depth of cut and repeat. Soon the same cut will be required with the router sliding down the bars. Continue in this way until the edge reaches the required thickness. This can be tested using a 'mullet', which has a groove the same width as the frame and can be tried

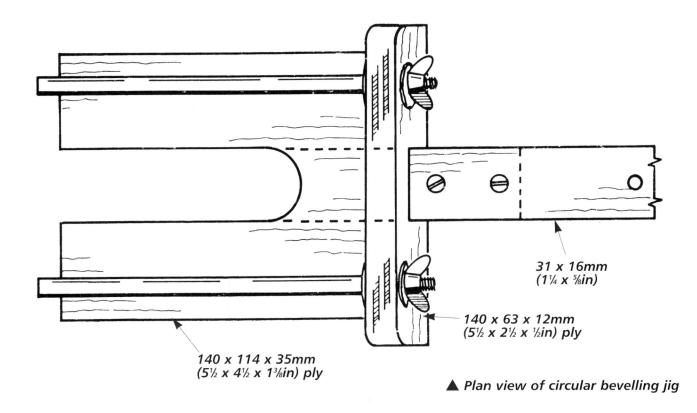

31 x 16mm
(1¼ x ⁵⁄₈in)

140 x 63 x 12mm
(5½ x 2½ x ½in) ply

140 x 114 x 35mm
(5½ x 4½ x 1³⁄₈in) ply

▲ *Plan view of circular bevelling jig*

Lightening the underside of a table top for example

Finishing with a smoothing plane may be required

on the edge of the panel. When happy with the fit, lock the depth stop at this setting.

Repeat on the other three sides of the panel. Make sure to complete with a very fine cut to obtain the best finish.

Step-fielding
On the step-fielding the angle will be found to be slightly under-cut. This can be squared off with a couple of fine cuts with a shoulder plane. Alternatively, change to a half-round cutter, but note that very precise setting will be required to produce this effect successfully.

The fieldings may require a fine cut with a block plane, followed by sanding. Sanding alone may not be enough. The abrasive paper must be used on the wood block, working along, not across the grain. Work down the grades of paper then polish suitably.

> ## "Make sure to complete with a very fine cut to obtain the best finish"

Circular bevelling and fielding
Though circular panels can be fielded, they are really very uncommon. However, circular table-tops frequently require bevelling on the underside to give a thinner edge and a lighter appearance.

This process was dealt with in detail in the feature in making a Shaker style table, so I will only deal with it briefly here.

The circular block holding the router bars is as described. The fence and stabiliser rail are no longer required, being replaced by the radial arm. This has 6mm holes spaced at about 1in. Finer adjustments are made by sliding the router along the bars.

The pivot block is held in place by double-sided tape. A 6mm screw serves as the actual pivot, and a wing-nut prevents the arm from accidentally slipping off.

▲ *A mullet for testing the edge thickness of a panel*

A hold-down system

The basic holding method

Taking the pain out of workbench clamping with a simple hold-down system

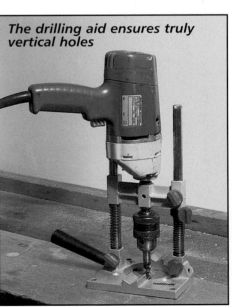

The drilling aid ensures truly vertical holes

▼ *Detail of the hold-down bolt*

THE 'bench holdfast' is the common method of holding work firmly to the benchtop while working it either by hand or with a router. Apart from the cost, of two hold-fasts, there is the inconvenience of making a number of large holes in the benchtop, probably of about ¾in in diameter, through which smaller items are likely to fall.

Some holdfasts are supplied with steel bushes, which are let in flush with the benchtop. Several of these on the work surface can prove quite a hazard to any edge tools coming into contact with them.

▲ *Holding for biscuit routing...*

▲ *...and for a stepped fielding. The batten acts as a fence*

"No-one likes to deface their benchtop, but holes of this small size will have no ill effects"

Bench work

However, there is another way to go about holding your work securely to the bench that costs very little and avoids the objections just described. A complete kit is made to my design and supplied by Vanguard Tools of Sheffield.

To set up, mark the centres of a row, or two rows of holes in the benchtop. I would suggest spacing them at about 8in between centres. No-one likes to deface their benchtop, but holes of this small size will have no ill effects.

▲ *Remember to site dowels or biscuits well clear of the fielding*

▼ *Fig 1 The holdfast*

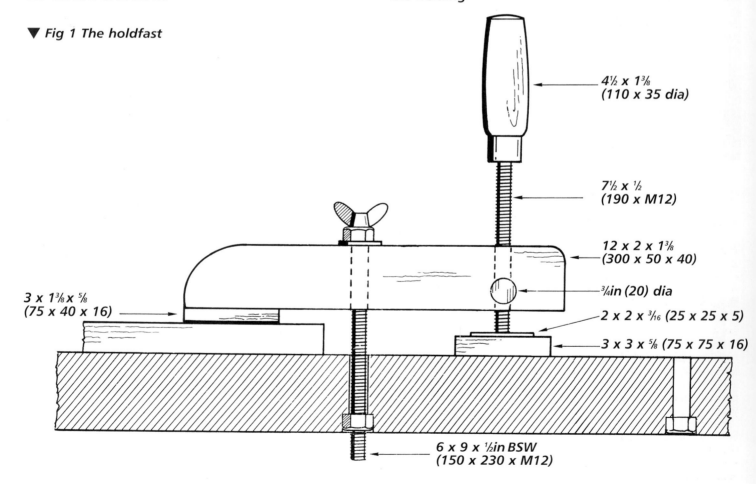

$4\frac{1}{2} \times 1\frac{3}{8}$
(110 x 35 dia)

$7\frac{1}{2} \times \frac{1}{2}$
(190 x M12)

$12 \times 2 \times 1\frac{3}{8}$
(300 x 50 x 40)

$\frac{3}{4}$in (20) dia

$2 \times 2 \times \frac{3}{16}$ (25 x 25 x 5)

$3 \times 3 \times \frac{5}{8}$ (75 x 75 x 16)

$3 \times 1\frac{3}{8} \times \frac{5}{8}$
(75 x 40 x 16)

$6 \times 9 \times \frac{1}{2}$in BSW
(150 x 230 x M12)

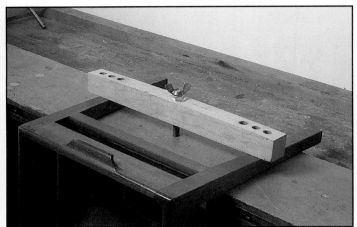

▲ *A single bolt holding helps to clean up a stool construction*

▲ *A homemade holdfast to work with the system*

On these centres, drill through 3mm pilot holes. A drilling aid is useful here as it guarantees a truly vertical hole. Now go to the underside of the benchtop and bore holes to accept the nuts supplied. The diameter is the size across the flats, which is also the same as the spanner size. The nearest size of an economical flatbit is ¾in.

On these pilot holes, drill to a depth of about 12mm, then from the top, on the same pilot, drill through at 13mm. Pull a nut into each cavity. Do not merely hammer in the nut, as this may damage the thread and will almost certainly drive the nut in askew. Instead, use a bolt, washer and bored wood block to do this.

The workpiece can be held in a number of ways. A useful method, for example, when using the router to biscuit joint, is to prepare two small hardwood blocks, bored about 14mm. These are used with two small off-cuts from the job.

"Do not merely hammer in the nut, as this may damage the thread"

Clamping battens

A further method, useful for panel fielding, and of course for other work, is the use of clamping battens. These are best made from hardwood, and can span two, three or more bench holes.

Drill holes to match, for instance, at 8in between centres. For ease of operation, bore these at 14mm. The batten simply clamps across the workpiece. In some situations the batten may also act as a fence for a plane or a power-router.

Stools and small tables can be held securely after the glue-up for cleaning up by plane, scraper or abrasive paper. One clamp is used centrally, but for larger work use two screws.

Morticing in the vice is generally viewed as a bad idea as it weakens the vice-fitting, and the work can be damaged by sliding down the vice jaws. A substantial block, retained for this job, can be bolted to the benchtop and the workpiece cramped to it. This is particularly useful on benches which have a front apron piece.

Single cramping

A holdfast can be made for single cramping, working on the principle of the handscrew. Slightly oversize holes will make for easier working. Position the holdfast using the centre screw, then apply pressure with the handled one. Aim to keep the tool as horizontal as possible.

Now about these holes, which nobody welcomes in the benchtop. Drop a piece of 12mm dowel into each hole, then plane flush with the benchtop. When a hole is required, the dowel can easily be pushed out with a pencil, or better still, a short piece of 8mm metal rod. Chisel a small facet on the entry end of the dowels; this will ensure that they always go in the same way.

A set of clamping two screws, with tommy bars, two large heavy washers and six nuts, are all available from Vanguard Tools, Sheffield (see Appendix, page 102 for more details). Further M12 nuts are available from all good hardware shops.

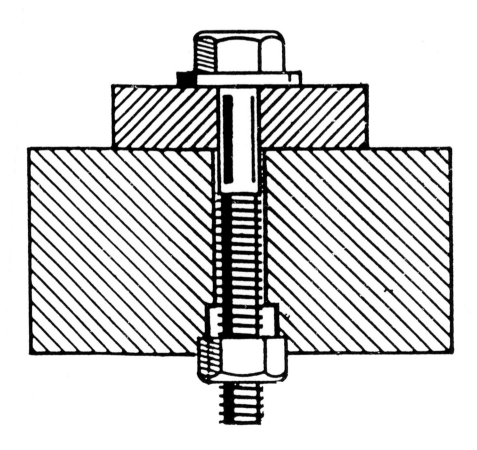

▲ *Fig 2 Draw the nut in with a bolt, don't hammer it in*

Routing multiple grooves

A fixed form jig for routing multiple housings

There are many ways to rout multiple grooves

THE applications for multiple grooving are both numerous and obvious: housings for shelves, both fixed and adjustable, housings for sliding trays and drawers, glass display shelves, and partitions in storage and filing systems are just a few.

Make sure you read the whole of this article before constructing any of these models, as useful tips are spread throughout to avoid repetition.

Fixed form jig

I shall begin with the simplest, fixed form.

Make a baseplate from ⅜in plywood or MDF, bore or rout a central hole and fix to the router base. Most routers have suitable holes which can be used, these are usually threaded M5 or M6. If you lack these, drill two holes and secure with countersunk screws and nuts.

Cramp a fence onto a piece of scrap material, and using the selected cutter, rout a shallow specimen groove. Carefully prepare a thin strip of hardwood to be a sweetly sliding fit in the groove.

Screw this, well countersunk, to the base with the required spacing between

the cutting edge of the router cutter and the strip. To begin it may be necessary to work the first groove from a cramped on fence, without using the jig.

From this point on it is only necessary to run the guide strip in the existing groove. Plunge to the pre-set depth stop and rout the groove or housing. Continue in this leapfrog manner.

Through grooves are easy. Stopped grooves can be achieved either by making an index mark on the edge of the base, or working right through and later gluing on an edging strip.

▲ *Details of the foot*

◀ *Underside of the fixed form jig*

▼ *Routing a housing with the foot jig*

"Check that the combined router and foot do not rock"

Guide strip

For this model, prepare a thickish foot, stand it and the router on a flat surface and mark the positions of the holes. This can be done easily by clamping two pencils or ballpoint pens in the routers as markers.

Drill ⁵⁄₁₆in holes, fit a pair of Vanguard router rods and assemble the router and fence on a flat surface. Check that all is well and that the combined router and foot do not rock.

Next, produce a hardwood guide strip to suit the pre-cut first groove. Screw it on using countersunk screws and you're done. In some cases a bright metal strip can be found which exactly matches the cutter.

▶ **Working a housing with the simple adjustable jig**

▼ **Foot to fit the housings with router rods**

▲ Top view of the more complex adjustable jig...

▲ ...and the under view

"There is another way to make an adjustable version"

Adjustable jigs

The final two models are adjustable versions, and I shall begin with the simplest. First make a block similar to a levelling foot. Gauge and carefully plane it down to thickness until it fits and slides easily in a pre-worked housing.

Either rout two slots to suit the router rods' spacing, or saw them and then glue on a substantial lipping. The common centre distance of 85mm suits the Bosch POF and Elu 96 routers. Make the slots ⁵⁄₁₆in to cover any slight inaccuracy.

Fit up the router with a pair of router rods and stand the router, with the cutter withdrawn, on the workpiece. Position the foot in the first housing, which will already have been worked, and assemble with the router. Set the router's depth stop then plunge and rout as described earlier.

There is another way to make an adjustable version. Begin by gluing a stout block to a plywood base. Mark the centres of the holes for the rods using the two pencils trick. Drill these oversize to about ⁵⁄₁₆in.

Assemble the router, rods and base, making sure that the router sits well on the base. Draw round the hole in the router's base, draw two parallels to this and cut out a sizable slot. Screw on a slide bar of suitable width.

Cut the first housing conventionally, adjust the router along the rods, set the depth slot and rout the housings.

Angled housing present no problems. Using the simple adjustable jig, begin by cutting the first housing using the common cramped-on batten as a fence, then proceed as before. When the angle is considerable, it helps to use a longer guide, so in this instance I find the more complex adjustable jig the most suitable and robust jig for the job.

▲ Working an angled housing with the simple adjustable jig

▼ Angled housings with the complex adjustable jig. Note the longer guide for the larger angle

Multiple mortices

Many ways of morticing with the router

THERE are several ways of morticing with the router, but this is one of the more permanent methods, and one of the best. Its success depends on using the Vanguard Router Rods, available from Vanguard Cutting Tools.

The basic woodwork

Bearers

I usually use good quality birch multi-ply, or, if you have objections to it, use MDF. The sizes shown are merely suggestions, but they suit the Bosch POF and the Elu MOF96 routers.

Prepare the baseplate to size and screw it to a block to be gripped in a vice. A square block permits the work to be fed in along or across the bench, whichever is more convenient for the job in hand.

Now prepare the bearers. The slots in these can be sawn or routed. For M6 threads cut these to 7mm to give ease of working. Assemble the bearers on the router rods to mark their position on the baseboard.

One bearer is fixed. Glue and screw this securely in place. Drill the removable bearer to take long M6 roofing bolts. To permit slight adjustment, drill at ¼in from the top, then 8mm most of the way from the base to connect.

To mark the centres of the holes on the baseboard, insert two 8mm dowel marker pins, assemble the bearers with the router rods in place and smartly tap with a hammer. To give easy movement when

Levelling up the router using parallel blocks

stout paper under them. Slacken the wing-nuts and drop the router base onto them. Clamp firmly.

Roughly fit the two fences and insert the appropriate cutter, using the longest cutter available. The morticer is not for really heavy work, so the long series cutters will generally do. For deeper mortices use engineers' end cutting milling cutters.

As these are only made parallel, light-weight routers will be restricted to ¼in. Wider mortices must be worked by taking two cuts at the timber.

Morticer skills

Set the router centrally on the rods, feed in a marked workpiece and plunge the router, not switched on, to grip it in the centre of the marked mortice. Bring up both fences and lock them in place finger tight. Any further small adjustments can be efficiently made by sliding the router along the bars.

Set the stop to the required depth. Plunge the router, making several cuts until full depth is reached. Take care not to burn, then cut a series of touching holes at full depth. Only then can the workpiece be moved along to remove the waste left between.

Obviously the standard router produces mortices with rounded ends. These can be chopped square with a hand chisel or, more commonly, the tenon ends can be rounded with a woodfile.

setting up, at this stage slip in thin card washers under the inside washers on one bearer. The difference this makes to subsequent adjustments will be obvious.

Drill fine pilot holes on the marks, about ¹⁄₁₆in or less. On the underside, drill shallow cavities of ¾in to take two M6 T-nuts. On the same centres, drill straight through at 8mm.

Never hammer in T-nuts as they are bound to go askew and the threads may be damaged. Instead, draw them in with a bolt, washer and wood block as shown.

Now assemble without the card washers. Check that the router bars will move freely up and down in the slots. Similarly bore and fit further T-nuts for the fences. Now prepare the fences, using good-quality ½in plywood with a solid wood fence. Gluing to edge plywood is not reliable at the best of times, so strengthen with two wood screws.

It is very important that the two fences are vertical, and that they will close together perfectly. The slots must naturally suit the T-nuts and should be made a trifle over-wide to give easy adjustment.

Assemble with 30mm M6 roofing bolts. If preferred, secure with plastic knobs, or make from wingnuts as shown. Screws will need more effort so they are less likely to be left slack.

Setting up

Set up for morticing as follows. Fit the bars onto the router, secure them in the fixed bearer, add the removable bearer and clamp. To fix the router height, slide in two identical workpieces with a slip of

The optimum set-up for morticing using a middleweight Elu 96 will guarantee great results

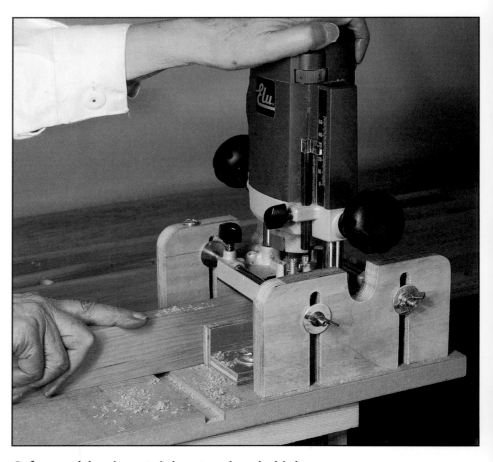

Safe morticing is certainly a two-handed job

An economical morticer to take Vanguard router rods

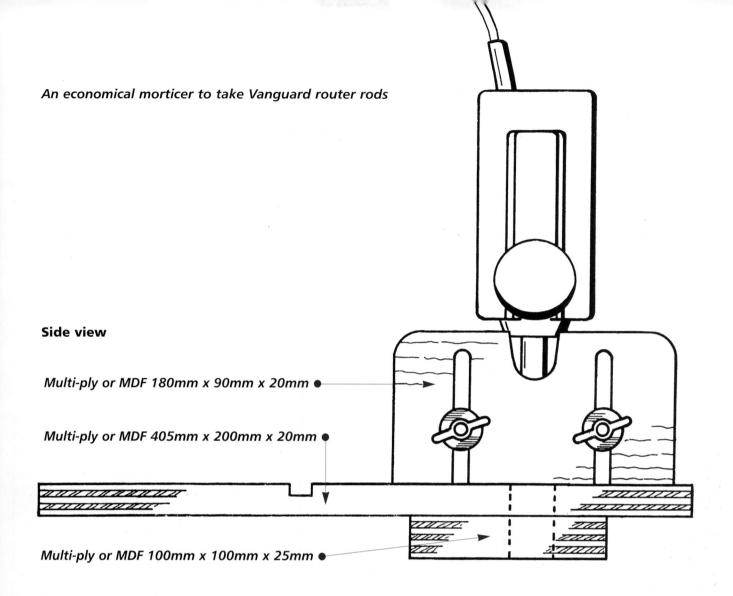

Side view

Multi-ply or MDF 180mm x 90mm x 20mm ●

Multi-ply or MDF 405mm x 200mm x 20mm ●

Multi-ply or MDF 100mm x 100mm x 25mm ●

Plan view

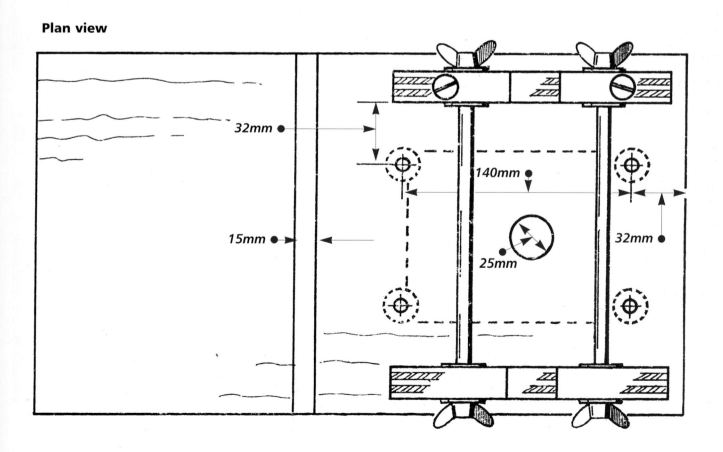

32mm ●

140mm ●

15mm ●

25mm

32mm ●

Cutting tenons

Using the same T-nuts, add a slotted length stop. The workpiece can be simply hand-held and fed across the cutter from left to right. The stop makes it impossible to cut too far.

For the best quality of jointing, saw the shoulders with a fine tenon saw. Deeply knife the shoulder line, then chisel a shallow groove in which to run the saw.

Better still, construct the simple cross-slide running in the groove on the baseplate. For this operation remove the fences. Drop the router and level it by inserting two workpieces.

Inset a workpiece, plunge the cutter to it and lock there. Remove the workpiece and increase the cut slightly. Using the cross-slide, feed in the workpiece against the rotation of the cutter, from left to right, starting at the end.

Check the tenon repeatedly in its mortice. If the tenon is not central, and most are, complete one side on all the components, then adjust and start on the other, continuing to test. End with a fine cut to give a good finish. With these sizes, tenons up to 2¾in wide can be formed.

In fitting tenons to their mortices very fine adjustment is often needed. If the router has only a simple depth stop, here is a way of achieving it. After making a cut, halt the router in that position on the job and lock it there.

Now raise the depth stop, insert a piece of stout paper and drop the depth stop onto it. Lock there. Now remove the paper and plunge the router to that setting for the next cut. Half lap-joints can be formed in the same way.

To work as a thicknesser, to rebate or mould, simply reverse the morticing fences as seen in the photograph. If you have graduated from a basic router to something more advanced, why not keep the original as a dedicated mortice and tenon machine?

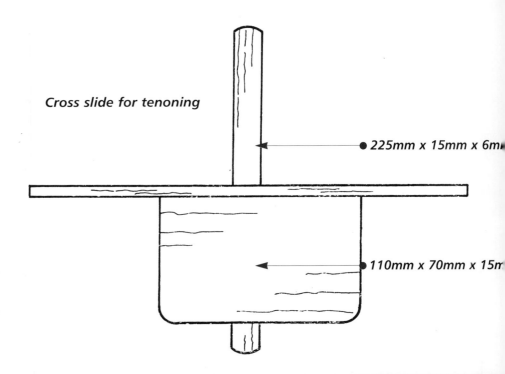

Cross slide for tenoning

• 225mm x 15mm x 6m

• 110mm x 70mm x 15m

The set-up for forming small tenons

Bob Wearing shows his unique method for cutting a tenon

Working Perspex

PLASTIC

Successfully cutting this innovative alternative to glass

PERSPEX is a material that we may need to work upon from time to time, maybe as a glass substitute or as part of a tool, jig or template. Fortunately, work is only required on the edges of this sometimes difficult medium. Convenient sources for this are firms making plastic signs, which you can find in the Yellow Pages. These firms, especially the small ones, are usually happy to dispose of their offcuts. I generally use clear or 'smoked' for most purposes, though a coloured opaque is sometimes handy.

Marking-out is best achieved by using a sharp awl or compass point and a steel rule or try square. A marking gauge is also handy but is inclined to suffer somewhat from the very sharp edges. The most common practice with Perspex is to saw, file and then work down through the grades of abrasive paper, but this is a rather tedious process. Here is an

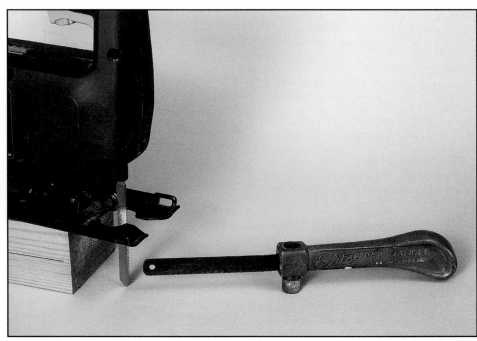

Jigsaw with fine metal cutting blade and hacksaw blade in pad handle

alternative, and, I think, a better method.

It is said that the best saw for Perspex is someone else's. This material is very bad for tenon and bandsaws, and circular saws splinter it. For short lengths of cutting I use a

sharp hacksaw blade in a pad handle, while longer cuts can be made with a small jigsaw fitted with a fine metal cutting blade. Better still is a scroll saw, with the workpiece supported on a piece of thin MDF.

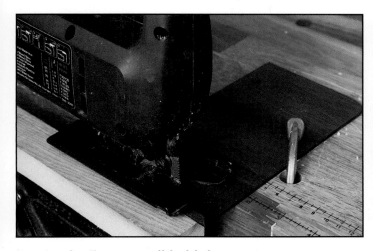

Sawing by jigsaw, well held down

A fine set scraper plane works quite sweetly

Planing follows sawing. Perspex rapidly dulls the plane blade and the 25° bevel gives rise to chattering. To successfully plane Perspex edges I suggest the following. Dig out an old, nearly worn out blade and on the flat side grind a very small bevel of about 80° and sharpen on this bevel. Set the cap iron well back, since it plays no part in this operation, being merely the means of adjusting the cut and the lateral position. Set a fine cut. Keep the plane square to the face and apply firm pressure. It is generally preferable to work in from both ends to prevent any breakout at the corners.

For longer pieces I sometimes use my planer, cutting with the ¼in of cutter away from the fence. This seems to do no harm. A finely set Stanley Scraper Plane No 80 works well on Perspex, and having a flat sole will produce a reasonably straight edge. I also find that a fine finish can be obtained with a freshly sharpened cabinet scraper (the simple blade type). This tool is particularly useful in removing the aggressively sharp arises and in cleaning up rounded edges so that the piece can be comfortably handled. In my opinion, having used this method, most readers will be satisfied with the results they get and will not wish to go further with abrasives.

By the way, keep the protective paper on the Perspex as long as possible. However, be aware that scrap and offcut material may have lost this.

Practise your drill
Centres can be marked with a punch, though tap gently, supporting the Perspex on a piece of thin MDF. Too much force may crack it. Wood drills do the job well since their needle point enables them to start precisely. If engineers' twist drills are used, drill a small pilot hole first, and then follow with bigger drills. Countersinking for screw heads can be done with any of the countersink drills now available.

One final warning! Check that the vice jaws are smooth and clean as any blemish here may get repeatedly etched on the Perspex, spoiling the work.

The finishing tools. Plane with specially modified cutter, cabinet scraper and Stanley scraper plane

Finishing with the cabinet scraper

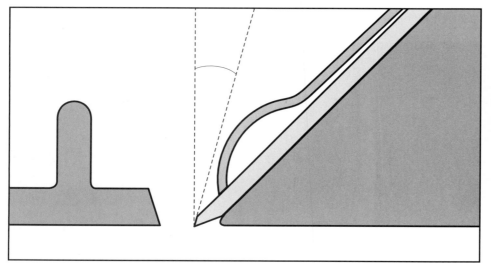

"Keep the protective paper on the Perspex as long as possible. However, be aware that scrap and offcut material may have lost this"

Routing over a gap

Using the router to ski-jump the gap

"The router can leap the gap with all the grace of a Klosters ski jumper"

The router on skis

"A router on skis" is, I think, an oft-coined expression by router expert Ron Fox. It is such an apt term for this technical trick that I have no hesitation in using it again. But why put your router on skis? Because with these attachments the router can leap across a cavity which is larger than the router's base, with all the grace of a Klosters ski jumper.

This situation occurred when I was building a router table. The actual tabletop was made from 19mm (¾in) MDF and I wanted to let in an aluminium plate about 3mm (⅛in) thick. This plate was considerably larger than the router's base since the unit would eventually be suspended from it. The plate needed to finish flush with the table surface so fine adjustment of the router was critical in obtaining a perfect fit.

I made the skis from material 32mm x 19mm (1¼ x ¾in) and 375mm (15in) long and fixed them on with the versatile Vanguard router rods.

To mark the positions of the holes, clamp two pencils into the router base and offer up the two skis. The average pencil fits quite nicely, which is a useful tip for other applications... Drill oversize at 8mm (⁵⁄₁₆in) to permit some slight adjustment. My first

Spanning a cavity larger than the router's base

thought was to stand the ski-kitted router on a flat surface while tightening everything up, but this turned out to be a bad idea as the wing-nuts and large repair washers would catch on the workpiece. To give clearance, therefore, stand the router on an offcut of 6mm (¼in) plywood, drop the skis to the flat surface and lock there.

Soften off all the corners until they are nice and smooth and then curve up the ends of the running faces like ski tips. If you think you'll be using your ski kit frequently then give them a couple of coats of sealer or varnish.

Readers will no doubt have their own further uses for the skis, one of which might be the letting into a table top of decorative ceramic tiles or a piece of Formica on which to stand hot tea or coffee pots.

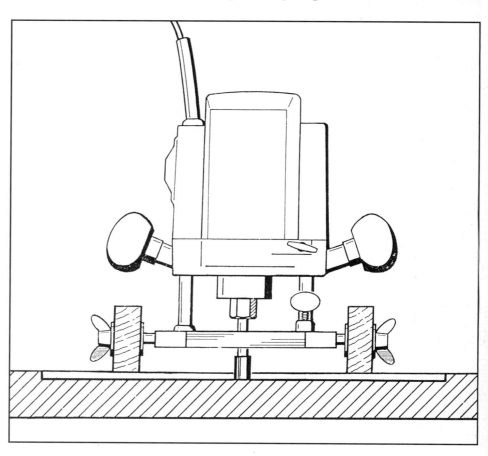

End grain clean-up

How to smooth over end-grain aggro

Smoothing over and generally calming-down what exactly? Well, all those protrusions that occur in end grain which normally have to be rather laboriously planed off. These include through tenons, through dovetails, keyed mitre joints, comb joints, through dowels and screwhead filler plugs.

Three methods are shown: choose whichever one is most suitable for the circumstances.

The simple form Model A
Make a base of 12mm (½in) multi-ply to suit the router's base. Bore a hole to match the central hole in the router base. Add two shaped blocks from 10mm (⅜in) plywood, which will be thick enough and simply glue them on. Soften all the corners and give a coat or two of sealer to keep the jig clean and smart-looking. Attach this base to the router base, using existing threaded holes or woodscrews through clear holes. On some routers it may be necessary to drill two holes for this. This method will be the same for all models.

Vanguard router rods Model B
This is, in effect, the levelling foot described above, but with an extra foot. Router rods are now threaded at both ends, making them even more versatile. The feet should be made from hardwood. The slots may be routed or made by sawing and then gluing on a closing strip. Assemble the router, bars and two feet. Fully withdraw the cutter. Stand the tool on a truly

"Three methods are shown: choose whichever one is most suitable for the circumstances"

An underside view of Model A

Using Model A to clean up protruding dowels

Using Model A to clean up through tenons

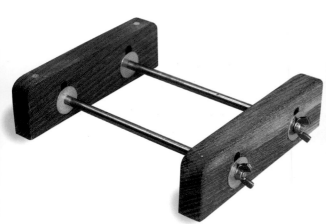

Vanguard router rods on Model B

Model B in action on through tenons

Model C base - for use on corners

flat surface. Insert a piece of, say, 12mm (½in) multi-ply under the router, slacken the wing nuts then drop the feet to the surface. Lock the wing nuts there. The tool is now ready for work.

For corner protrusions Model C

These will include dovetails, keys of mitred joints and comb joints where the router must considerably overhang the workpiece. This calls for a different technique altogether. Make a long base from 12mm (½in) multi-ply, shape one end to the router and bore a large central hole to suit. Then glue on a shorter sole of 10mm (⅜in) ply. Shape the other end and attach a knob, either turned up or bought in. Soften all the sharp edges, sand and seal and then fix the router to the base.

Using the tools

Fit a largish end cutting router bit, for example, 12mm (½in) or more. Stand the tool on a level surface. Insert a piece of paper under the cutter and then plunge the router onto it. Lock it there. The protrusions can now be routed away, leaving the paper thickness to be removed by a sharp smoothing plane. Make sure you are cutting into the rotation of the cutter and as far as possible inwards from the edge. Don't try to do the whole job by router as the surface is bound to be scored. When using Model C keep a good downward pressure on your knob.

The complete Model C

Cleaning up a keyed mitre joint with Model C

Another version of the Model B

Cross halving joints

Teetering on the workbench is resolved with a foot for support

Cross halvings, as in Fig 1, are generally sawn and chopped out by hand. However, when a number are required, for instance when making a grille, the router can speed up the job. Generally it's wise to saw the sides, knock out the waste with a chisel, then level everything precisely with the router. Obviously the router cannot sit effectively on a thin edge of say 20mm (³/4in), so a levelling foot is required to keep the router stable.

Cramp it up

Cramp the workpiece to the benchtop or to a batten bolted to the benchtop. Fit the router bars and the levelling foot then stand the router on two workpieces, or on one and its offcut. Slacken the wing nuts to allow the foot to drop to the benchtop and lock it there.

Waste removal machine

Remove the remaining waste in stages until the required depth is reached. Set the depth stop there, then repeat on all the other similar components. For a wider housing, such as in Fig 2, saw the ends for accuracy and safety. On a housing of appreciable width the entire waste can be removed by routing. The length of the workpiece and the number of housings or halvings present no problems.

Mais oui, Rodders

Router rods are available directly from the makers: Vanguard Cutting Tools, Sheffield (see Appendix, page 102) for approximately £5 per pair for 8mm diameter and 10mm sizes.

Routing a Cross Halving showing the holding method

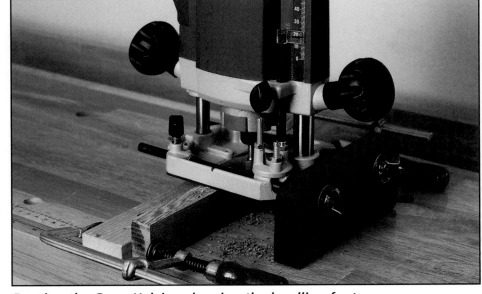

Routing the Cross Halving showing the levelling foot

Fig. 1

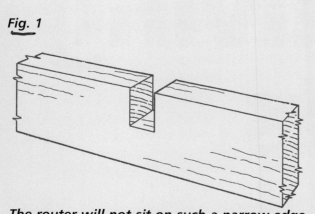

The router will not sit on such a narrow edge. A levelling foot is essential

Fig. 2

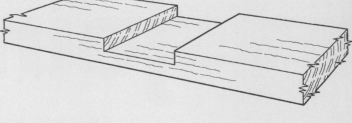

Flat halving joints.
Wide halving can be routed unaided.
Narrow halvings require the levelling foot.

"Obviously the router cannot sit effectively on a thin edge of say 20mm (3/4in), so a levelling foot is required to keep the router stable. "

Fig 4 Routing the Cross Halving

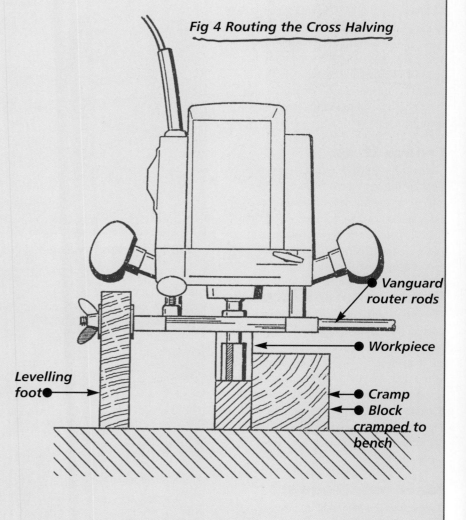

Vanguard router rods

Workpiece

Cramp
Block cramped to bench

Levelling foot

Fig. 3 The levelling foot

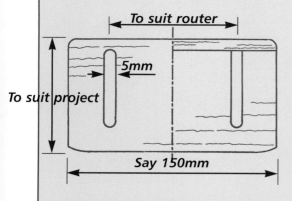

To suit router

5mm

To suit project

Say 150mm

The slots: rout or bore, saw and glue on a strip

No sizes are critical, use available material

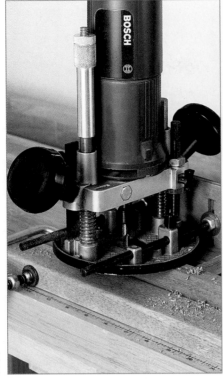

The holding arrangement

Details of the levelling foot

MORTICED

Stability and simplicity are the guiding words for tackling morticing by router

Without the levelling root it is impossible to settle the router on a narrow edge such as is shown in the photographs. For all but the smallest components, it will be necessary to make a levelling foot much taller than has been used so far – tall enough to meet the present needs. After a while, a small collection of levelling feet will accumulate.

Either rout the slots or saw them and then glue on a strip. For morticing, a fence is also required. Make this from 10mm (3/8in) material, the same length as the foot.

This fence is screwed to the foot through the slots with long woodscrews using large washers under the heads (the washers are sold as repair washers or mudguard washers). The width is not really important; use what is available.

Fit a long series cutter with end-cutting capacity. Good alternatives are engineers' milling cutters. These have parallel shanks so only the 1/4in will fit the smaller routers. However, wider mortices can be produced using two cuts.

Set and begin

Adjust the fence to the marked mortice, set the depth stop and begin. Plunge to make a series of holes the length of the mortice. Only then take several traversing cuts, finishing to depth. To plunge and then to traverse is liable to break the cutter.

Either trim the round ends of the mortices square, or round the ends of the tenons with a wood file, which is easier. Any length of material can be morticed in this way on the benchtop.

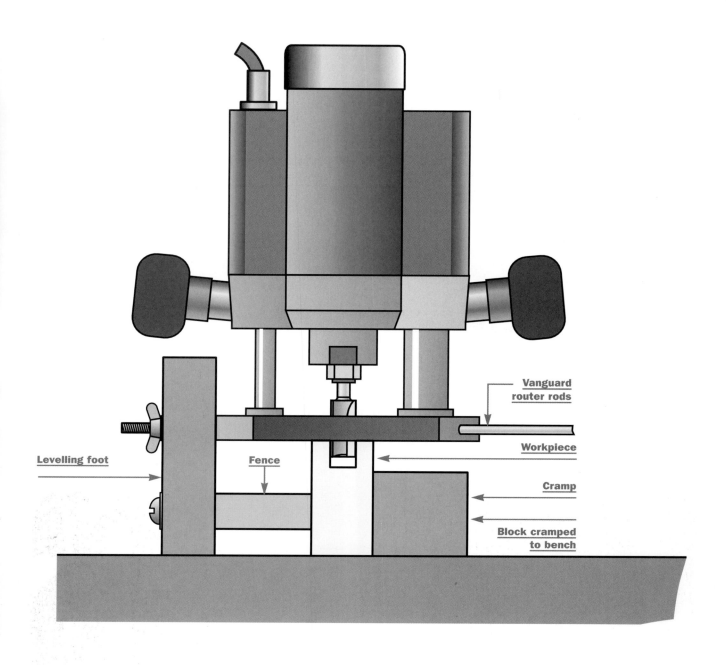

Vanguard router rods

Workpiece

Cramp

Block cramped to bench

Levelling foot

Fence

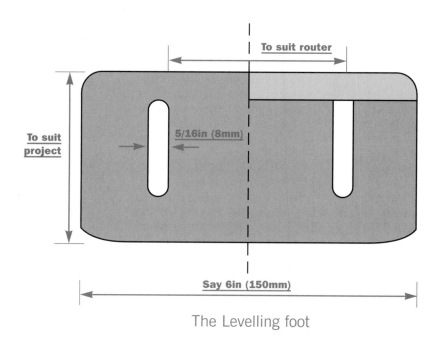

To suit router

To suit project

5/16in (8mm)

Say 6in (150mm)

The Levelling foot

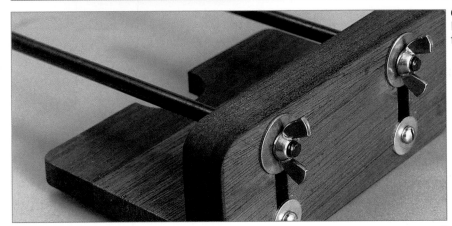

LONG BITS

What do you do when timber is too big to handle?
The answers are here

This particular aid was developed to satisfy the need to produce some skirting board. The length was long, but the width was narrow, giving a small surface on which to settle the router. Even working on wider components, there is always the chance of the router canting over.

If this happens, the bad cut will always be into the job, never into the waste. Also, the fence supplied may be thicker than the workpiece. Overhanging the bench edge is not much help since the vice forms an obstruction.

You may not have a router table or may only have one of the small commercial models. Long lengths of timber fit uneasily on these. Long components can, however, be conveniently worked on the bench using this simple aid.

The requirements are a pair of Vanguard router rods, a levelling foot and a fence. By now you may have collected several levelling feet. Select an appropriate one. Make a fence to suit. Sizes are not critical, so choose to suit the job in hand and the available material.

The fence will need a cavity to accept the cutter. This can be sawn out but boring is easier. I used an expansive machine bit set at 38mm (1 ¹/₂in). Make the fence extra wide and saw off, or bore just over half a hole. This is easy on a drilling machine, but note that the workpiece must be clamped down.

down to business

Drill two pilot holes for the No 8 round head woodscrews. Attach to the fence using washers to span the slots. I find the packs of washers sold for use with pop rivets are useful for this kind of job. If satisfactory, remove the fence for the time being.

Set up the router bars and levelling foot, then stand the router on the workpiece and an offcut. This keeps the router stable while the levelling foot is dropped to the benchtop and locked there.

Fit the appropriate cutter in the chuck. I find the simple type of cutter as in Fig A is preferable to the type in Fig B since if the workpiece is thin, the nut will foul the benchtop and prevent the required setting.

Re-attach the fence and set for the job in hand. Small mouldings in soft woods can be worked in one pass. If two or more cuts are required, adjust by using the plunge, with the depth stop set for the final cut. Components of any length can be worked in this way.

Clamp the workpiece firmly to the bench and work just under a bench length at a time. Then slide along and repeat. The junction will be invisible.

When a cutter with a bearing must be used, components up to say 75mm (3in) can be worked by clamping the workpiece on its edge and using a taller levelling foot. A stock of levelling feet will eventually be built up.

rebating

This is a somewhat similar process. Long rebates are often required to hold and mask the edges of plywood panels and skirting boards, sometimes to accept electric cable.

Rebating cutters without a bearing are required since they have no nut to obstruct. The width of the rebate is infinitely variable. Set up exactly as before, controlling the finished depth by means of the depth stop. If there is a revolving turret depth stop arrangement, as on the small Elu routers, set a first cut and a finer finishing cut.

Control the width of the rebate by sliding the router along the router bars. Set the fence as low as possible on the levelling foot, but just clear of the bench top.

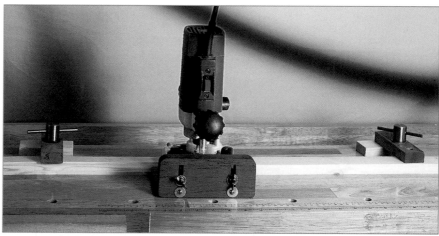
Routing a long component by stages

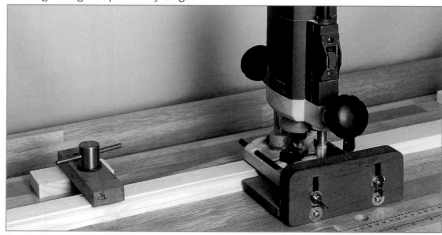
Routing a long narrow component, showing the hold-down arrangement

Close-up of the process

Detail of the Vanguard hold-down system. The kit consists of two clamp screws with washers and six nuts. The woodwork is workshop- made

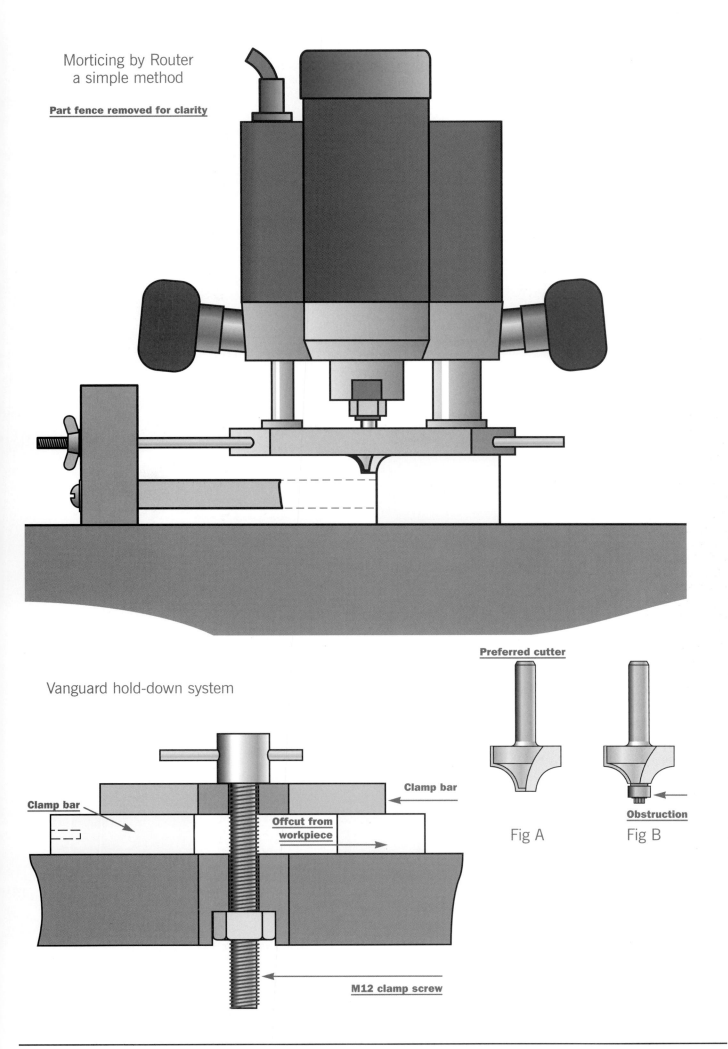

Morticing by Router
a simple method

Part fence removed for clarity

Vanguard hold-down system

Clamp bar

Clamp bar

Offcut from
workpiece

M12 clamp screw

Preferred cutter

Fig A

Obstruction

Fig B

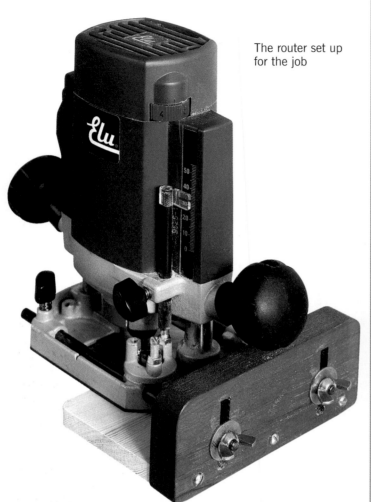

The router set up for the job

ROUTING the waste

Bob Wearing explains how to remove waste from the sockets of lap or drawer dovetails

The levelling foot with a fence attached

Routing the waste from dovetail sockets

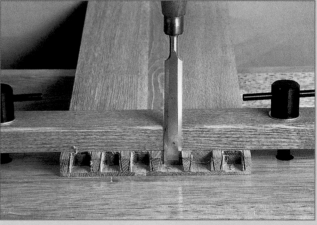

Clearing the corners using the paring fence

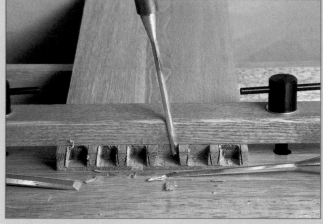

Undercutting the corners with a special dovetail chisel

Removing the waste

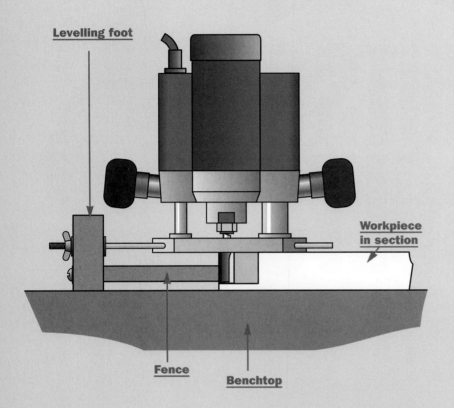

Levelling foot

Workpiece in section

Fence

Benchtop

The Levelling foot

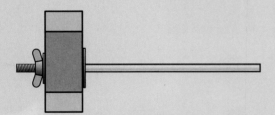

Slots can be routed or built up

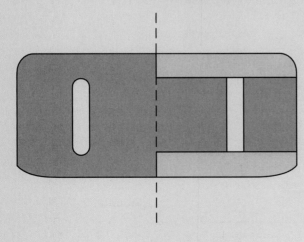

emoving waste is the tedious part of cutting the lap or drawer dovetail, so any mechanisation is more than welcome. Again the router comes to the rescue, but with less than half of the router base on the workpiece, it is unstable. Fortunately the levelling foot remedies this. With the foot set for the thickness of the workpiece, there is no chance of the router rocking. Now a fence is needed to prevent cutting in too far.

Take a small offcut which must be slightly thinner than the workpiece and screw it to the levelling foot, raised so as to just clear the bench top. Generally the existing slots are inconvenient so it is better to drill holes specifically for this fence. Depending on the thickness of the workpiece, smaller washers may be required on the inside of the rods.

The width of the fence is important and can only be decided by measuring the base. When using my Elu 96 MOF router I find 82mm (3^1/$_4$in) a convenient width (see both diagrams.)

Adjust the fence to prevent over cutting. It is safe to rout right up to the shoulder line which will be cut precisely. Plunge in several stages until the finished depth is reached. Lock the depth stop there. Repeat this exercise for all the other sockets. There is no need to leave a bit to be removed by chisel as a good and accurate finish will have been obtained.

Using a chisel, trim the corners of the sockets back to the line. An accurate shoulder line is guaranteed by the use of a paring fence. Plane a true edge on a hardwood fence and glue several pieces of glasspaper to the underside. Clamp this in place to guide the chisel.

FINISHING THE SOCKETS

The best way to clean up the corners is with a pair of special dovetailing chisels. Ashley Iles made me a pair of ^{1}/$_4$in skew chisels, both a left and a right hand. They were ground at an angle of one in six. These will clean up the corners without excessive cutting into the lap. It is more effective to remove the waste with a thin straight cutter than a dovetail cutter. This latter will leave much more waste in the corners and is unlikely to match the dovetail angle already chosen. It will also undercut at the shoulder line rendering its usage pointless.

NUTS & BOLTS

for Routing Aids

Photo A (back left to right) Roofing bolt, Hexagonal head bolt, Carriage bolt, Tee nuts, Hexagon nut, wing-nuts, (front) Standard washer, Large washer, Repair washer

L ike many other writers in the woodworking world, I have over the years written about a great number of jigs and aids for the router. The one thing we all need is a collection of fixings, holdings and other clamping devices.

While some of these devices can be purchased if a good tool shop is near at hand, many of us have to make our own. For those of us who do, here are some of the vital ingredients.

BITS & BOBS

Screwed metal rod is now commonly available, not only in tool shops but from general ironmongers. Metric, M4, M6, M8, etc is sold in metre lengths. BSW, (British Standard Whitworth), 1/4in, 5/16in, 3/8in and comes in 3ft lengths. BSW is a coarser, faster thread, so it tightens quicker.

Nuts are either square and thin and rather crudely made, or hexagonal which are thicker and machined. Thin hexagonal

nuts are manufactured but not easily found. If they are let into the wood, square nuts have the better grip although hexagon nuts, when pulled in, are quite adequate. When boring to pull in hexagon nuts, choose a bit which exactly fits the appropriate spanner.

Wing-nuts of course match the threads. They can be used loose, accompanied with a washer for wood, or fixed to make thumbscrews. Brazing or welding a wingnut to a piece of screwed rod brings in the element of heat. This produces fire scale, which can be avoided by fixing the wingnut with a thin lock-nut, Meccano-wise. I have found this method satisfactory and have used it for making thumbscrews for some years.

The older, cruder cast iron wingnuts give a better purchase than the smarter modern variety. Recently, however, I have discovered an adhesive called HafiXs. A mere drop of this will secure a wingnut to a screwed rod. Thus far I have not managed to dislodge one. At £10 for 20g this is not cheap but there is a refrigerator shelf life of five years. So far, by various repairs, I have recouped the cost. Metal, glass, or almost any material in small sizes can be successfully bonded together. I am sure I will find further uses for it when it comes to jig making.

Talking of uses, the various bolts have theirs. The basic hexagon head bolt in addition to holding components together, is essential for drawing in bolts and Tee nuts. If these are hammered in it is probable that they will go in askew or that the thread will be damaged.

The carriage bolt has a square under the head which successfully prevents it from turning. Roofing bolts are now freely obtainable in a vast range of sizes. Like the best carriage bolts they are zinc plated, which looks good and resists corrosion. When put into a suitable threaded hole, these will not rotate. Short lengths of screwed rod are also sometimes convenient in a threaded hole.

Few woodworkers will possess a set of engineers' taps and tap wrenches as their expense is hard to justify when considering the small amount of work they will be used for. Taps suitable for wood only can actually be made from screwed rod. Simply cut to length then file four tapered flats and add a wingnut. For a good fixing into wood, tap only until the tip comes through the workpiece, producing a tapered thread. Then, using two locked nuts, force the screwed rod into the hole. It should be sufficiently tight for most purposes.

Tee nuts come to us from the knock-down furniture industry. They are extremely useful for use with clamping screws. The available sizes seem to be M6, M8, 3/4in and 5/16in. Larger sizes are made, used and readily available, but I have yet to find a supplier of small quantities.

To fit these bore a shallow recess to take the flange, then on the same centre go through to accept the barrel. Tee nuts must never be hammered in. They should be drawn in, using a bored wood block, washer and hexagon head bolt.

To salvage Tee nuts from an abandoned jig, screw in a bolt in the barrel side and then tap out.

Washers appear in three forms and must

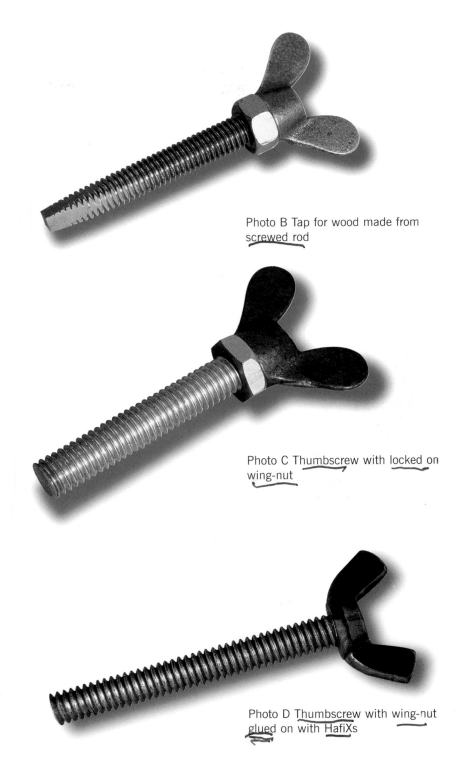

Photo B Tap for wood made from screwed rod

Photo C Thumbscrew with locked on wing-nut

Photo D Thumbscrew with wing-nut glued on with HafiXs

"The basic hexagon head bolt in addition to holding components together, is essential for drawing in bolts and Tee nuts."

always be used between wood and a nut or wing-nut. The engineering type is the smallest and should generally be avoided. I have found that a larger version spreads the pressure on the wood much better.

The most useful washer is variously called a multitude of names including a repair washer, a mudguard washer or a penny washer, the latter name coming from the pre-metrication days when a penny measured 1 1/4in.

When drilling for bolts and screws always use the brad pointed wood drill as opposed to the stubby pointed engineers twist drill as it will start precisely. For moving screws or moving components, enlarge the hole slightly with a twist drill to give an easy motion.

F E N C

View of the fence from the rear showing the adjusting screw and the spring

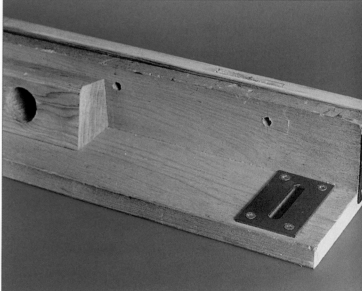

View from the rear showing the block to take the dust extractor hose and hinging

A fine adjusting fence for the router table

I imagine, from the numerous conversations I've had on the subject, that the majority of router tables are homemade ie: built in the workshop. I also believe that in most cases fine fence adjustment is achieved by a gentle tap to or from the cutter. There is a more precise way of going about this however, requiring less effort and materials. Here's how.

Prepare, from a piece of well seasoned hardwood, a second fence of the same dimensions as the existing fence. Join the two by a good butt hinge. Long screws are required to go into the end grain. Unscrew and mark out for drilling. Drill a shallow cavity of 19mm (3/4in) into the fixed fence

and then use an 8mm or 5/16in drill to go through.

Pull in a Tee Nut, either an M6 or 1/4in, using a bolt and large washer. Do not hammer it in as either the thread will be damaged or it will go in askew. The best way to avoid this is to prepare a thumbscrew. To avoid a heat process and the subsequent cleaning up, cut off a piece of screwed rod of the required length, round the end and attach a wing-nut by means of a thin lock-nut to secure it. Those of you au fait with Meccano will remember doing this. Alternatively an old radio knob can be used. Add a free wing-nut and a washer.

Cut out a cavity to clear the cutter and

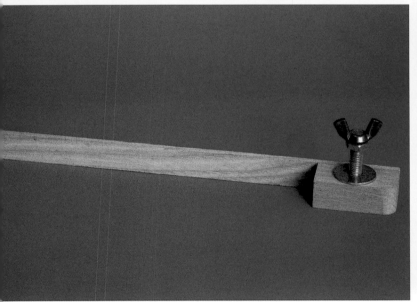

Details of the 'hold-down' springs

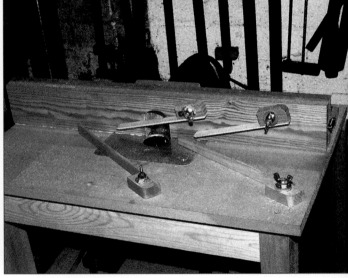

Springs in position on fence

provide an airway for chip extraction. This will match the cavity in the original fence. Put in two round head screws at the other end and attach a small coil spring. Elastic bands twisted round the screw will suffice. Let in a countersunk screw onto which the adjusting screw can bed. Then re-assemble.

To use, provisionally adjust the fence as previously done. Make the final adjustment using the screw. To prevent the screw moving as a result of vibration, tighten up the free wing-nut. Bear in mind that on a router table there is absolutely no need for the fence to be parallel to the edge of the table.

Two hold-downs can be fitted to the moving fence. To allow for this, bore two shallow depressions of 22mm (7/8in) diameter on the inside and then bore right through by 10mm (25/64in). Pull in two M8 Tee Nuts as previously described. The hold-down fingers are made by gluing springy laths of straight grained Ash, say 1 x 1/8in, to blocks bored at 8 or 8.5mm.

Thumbscrews with 8mm repair washers hold them in place. These are made as described before. Possibly, a similar pair of springs will have been made, screwing into the table, which hold the workpiece to the fence. As with many router aids, I now wonder how I ever managed without it.

> "As with many router aids, I now wonder how I ever managed without it."

MODERN DOWEL JOINTING

The correct way of dowel jointing

Drilling the dowel holes on a drilling machine.

Rear view showing the drilling aid.

You can pay quite a price for a dowelling jig. There are textbooks that give advice on making dowelled joints but they generally use a brace and bit. There is, however, an easier way.

This system applies only for jointing boards, sometimes called a widening joint, as for example in the making of a table top. It will not make substitutes for the mortice and tenon joint of say the flat frame.

The vital requirements are a drilling machine or an electric drill in a substantial drill stand, the correct drill for wood, sometimes called a lip and spur drill, and a set of dowel marker pins. (Interestingly the pins are a Victorian revival - as students just after the war, we made our own.)

As usual, a jig is needed. This can be made from MDF or muiti-ply; 3/4in or 19mm is most desirable as it gives a bit of weight. House a vertical working face into a baseboard. This gives a small lip which prevents accidental tipping over. To guarantee accuracy, place a triangular fillet inside. The whole thing can be glued and screwed together.

PREPARING THE JOINT

Now prepare the joint. I find a planer does the job quite satisfactorily, certainly for joints up to 1 metre. Select the true faces of the two boards, then for each joint plane one component with its true face to the fence of the planer and the other with its true face away from the fence. This compensates for any inaccuracy in the 90° setting of the fence.

Try to arrange it so that when jointed, both components plane well in the same direction. While this is not always possible, it is desirable.

Now mark the dowel centres on one workpiece. They can be quite randomly spaced and should be approximately on the centre line. No elaborate gauging and squaring is necessary as precise accuracy is unimportant. Time is saved by this method. Avoid spacing dowels where working will take place later, as for instance a fielded panel. Stab the centres with a small awl.

Set up the drilling machine and cramp the workpiece to the drilling jig, with the true face inwards. Now drill all the holes to a depth of just over half the length of the dowels to be used. It is likely that precut manufactured dowels will be used, so slightly countersink the holes and insert the dowel marker pins.

Lay the drilled workpiece on a flat surface up against some form of stop. Bring up the other component, line up for length and give several sharp taps with the hammer.

The centres have now been marked on the second board. Set it up in the jig, and drill on the marked centres. Slightly countersink these to leave space for exuded glue.

Notice that the drilling jig is not cramped to the drilling table. Check that the combined depth of the holes is deeper than the dowel length.

The joint can now be glued up. It must, of course, be cramped. If using three or more sash cramps, arrange them to be on alternate sides.

Clean-up follows normal procedure.

> "There are textbooks that give advice on making dowelled joints but they generally use a brace and bit."

The dowel marker pins inserted.

Applying a primer coat of PVA and water mix

VENEERING

The best way of veneering

Veneering is not one of those wood-working processes that the amateur rushes into. In many cases it can be avoided by the use of pre-veneered plywood. However, if it cannot be avoided, as is often case, do not despair, for there is hope!

The method I use has served me well over the years and is particularly useful for small work, requiring neither experience nor skill. That smelly old glue pot, never particularly welcome on the kitchen cooker, is not required any more. The same can be said of the expensive modern electric glue kettle designed for use in the workshop. The basis of all this is PVA adhesive.

This method appears to have been thought up in the 1960s by UNIBOND. It works with other makes of PVA glues, but always try them out before committing them to an actual job.

THE METHOD OF WORK

Cut the veneer to working size, ie slightly over the finished size. Tape the ends to prevent curling. It will be helpful if the ground is lightly toothed, either with a proper toothing plane, or by scraping with a hacksaw blade.

Mix a priming coat of adhesive consisting of one part of PVA and five parts of water. Stir and mix thoroughly, then apply to the inside face of the veneer and the surface. Cover the surfaces well, but remember not to make it too wet as this will cause excessive curling. Allow to dry naturally.

As I mentioned, the bonding solution consists of five parts of PVA with one part of water. This dilution is to ease the brushing on. The bonding solution should never be weaker than three parts of PVA

Ensure the iron is not too hot or the veneer will shrink and crack

A heavy cold cast iron is used to finish the process

with one part of water. There seems, however, no convincing reason to depart from the 5 + 1 mix. Again, coat both surfaces and allow to dry overnight.

When dry, lightly rub down with fine abrasive paper to remove any nibs or little high spots. With careful brushing in a non dusty room, there should be very little of this to do.

The next step is to carefully place the veneer in position, with treated surfaces together. If necessary, hold in position with a few strips of tape. Note, and this is very important, that the only tape to be used for veneering is of the gummed paper variety.

Veneering tape, which is not easy to find, is essentially an expensive, perforated form of gummed paper tape. Masking tape, drafting tape, plastic tape, carpet tape and even sellotape, are all to be avoided because of the mess they form when heated.

IRONING ON

Heat is applied by the ordinary domestic iron, set to wool. Iron through a piece of clean brown paper. Two things to be avoided are the use of newsprint and steam irons. However, if there is no alternative to the latter, check and double check that it's not steaming and press slowly.

In view of the heat retained in the material to be veneered, some form of rapid cooling is recommended. I use a cast-iron antique, kept cool by standing on the concrete floor. As soon as the veneer seems to be well ironed on, rapidly run over with the cool iron.

Any joints in the veneer, having been cut true, should be taped together before the start. When ironing, always work towards the joint. Excessive heat will cause the veneer to shrink and the joint to open, so use as little as possible while making sure it will do the job throughout. Check for any slight bubbles by tapping with the finger nails and, if present, repeat the process.

PVA stored in tins can pick up iron salts. These may react with the tannin in some veneers and cause dark staining. So, if in a tin, I would advise decanting on opening into a plastic container.

Finally, remember that material veneered on one side only will inevitably warp. This can be overcome by placing a cheaper balancing veneer on the other side.

Appendix

For further information on tools featured in this book, for example, router rods, depth gauge metal components and hold-down clamping systems, contact Vanguard Cutting Tools, who can supply their products by mail order worldwide:

Vanguard Cutting Tools
102 Harvest Lane
Sheffield
S3 8EG

Tel: 0114–2737677
Website: www.vanguardtools.com
Email: info@vanguardtools.com

Because the price of individual items is subject to change, up-to-date prices can be given upon application.

TITLES AVAILABLE FROM
GMC Publications

BOOKS

WOODCARVING

Beginning Woodcarving   *GMC Publications*
Carving Architectural Detail in Wood: The Classical Tradition
    Frederick Wilbur
Carving Birds & Beasts   *GMC Publications*
Carving the Human Figure: Studies in Wood and Stone   *Dick Onians*
Carving Nature: Wildlife Studies in Wood   *Frank Fox-Wilson*
Carving on Turning   *Chris Pye*
Decorative Woodcarving   *Jeremy Williams*
Elements of Woodcarving   *Chris Pye*
Essential Woodcarving Techniques   *Dick Onians*
Lettercarving in Wood: A Practical Course   *Chris Pye*
Making & Using Working Drawings for Realistic Model Animals
    Basil F. Fordham
Power Tools for Woodcarving   *David Tippey*
Relief Carving in Wood: A Practical Introduction   *Chris Pye*
Understanding Woodcarving in the Round   *GMC Publications*
Useful Techniques for Woodcarvers   *GMC Publications*
Woodcarving: A Foundation Course   *Zoë Gertner*
Woodcarving for Beginners   *GMC Publications*
Woodcarving Tools, Materials & Equipment (New Edition in 2 vols.)
    Chris Pye

WOODTURNING

Adventures in Woodturning   *David Springett*
Bowl Turning Techniques Masterclass   *Tony Boase*
Chris Child's Projects for Woodturners   *Chris Child*
Colouring Techniques for Woodturners   *Jan Sanders*
Contemporary Turned Wood: New Perspectives in a Rich Tradition
    Ray Leier, Jan Peters & Kevin Wallace
The Craftsman Woodturner   *Peter Child*
Decorating Turned Wood: The Maker's Eye   *Liz & Michael O'Donnell*
Decorative Techniques for Woodturners   *Hilary Bowen*
Illustrated Woodturning Techniques   *John Hunnex*
Intermediate Woodturning Projects   *GMC Publications*
Keith Rowley's Woodturning Projects   *Keith Rowley*
Making Screw Threads in Wood   *Fred Holder*
Turned Boxes: 50 Designs   *Chris Stott*
Turning Green Wood   *Michael O'Donnell*
Turning Pens and Pencils   *Kip Christensen & Rex Burningham*
Useful Woodturning Projects   *GMC Publications*
Woodturning: Bowls, Platters, Hollow Forms, Vases,
    Vessels, Bottles, Flasks, Tankards, Plates   *GMC Publications*
Woodturning: A Foundation Course (New Edition)   *Keith Rowley*
Woodturning: A Fresh Approach   *Robert Chapman*
Woodturning: An Individual Approach   *Dave Regester*
Woodturning: A Source Book of Shapes   *John Hunnex*
Woodturning Jewellery   *Hilary Bowen*

Woodturning Masterclass   *Tony Boase*
Woodturning Techniques   *GMC Publications*

WOODWORKING

Advanced Scrollsaw Projects   *GMC Publications*
Beginning Picture Marquetry   *Lawrence Threadgold*
Bird Boxes and Feeders for the Garden   *Dave Mackenzie*
Celtic Carved Lovespoons: 30 Patterns   *Sharon Littley & Clive Griffin*
Celtic Woodcraft   *Glenda Bennett*
Complete Woodfinishing   *Ian Hosker*
David Charlesworth's Furniture-Making Techniques
    David Charlesworth
David Charlesworth's Furniture-Making Techniques – Volume 2
    David Charlesworth
The Encyclopedia of Joint Making   *Terrie Noll*
Furniture-Making Projects for the Wood Craftsman   *GMC Publications*
Furniture-Making Techniques for the Wood Craftsman   *GMC Publications*
Furniture Restoration (Practical Crafts)   *Kevin Jan Bonner*
Furniture Restoration: A Professional at Work   *John Lloyd*
Furniture Restoration and Repair for Beginners   *Kevin Jan Bonner*
Furniture Restoration Workshop   *Kevin Jan Bonner*
Green Woodwork   *Mike Abbott*
Intarsia: 30 Patterns for the Scrollsaw   *John Everett*
Kevin Ley's Furniture Projects   *Kevin Ley*
Making Chairs and Tables   *GMC Publications*
Making Chairs and Tables – Volume 2   *GMC Publications*
Making Classic English Furniture   *Paul Richardson*
Making Heirloom Boxes   *Peter Lloyd*
Making Little Boxes from Wood   *John Bennett*
Making Screw Threads in Wood   *Fred Holder*
Making Shaker Furniture   *Barry Jackson*
Making Woodwork Aids and Devices   *Robert Wearing*
Mastering the Router   *Ron Fox*
Pine Furniture Projects for the Home   *Dave Mackenzie*
Practical Scrollsaw Patterns   *John Everett*
Router Magic: Jigs, Fixtures and Tricks to
    Unleash your Router's Full Potential   *Bill Hylton*
Router Tips & Techniques ✔   *Robert Wearing*
Routing: A Workshop Handbook   *Anthony Bailey*
Routing for Beginners   *Anthony Bailey*
Sharpening: The Complete Guide   *Jim Kingshott*
Sharpening Pocket Reference Book   *Jim Kingshott*
Simple Scrollsaw Projects   *GMC Publications*
Space-Saving Furniture Projects   *Dave Mackenzie*
Stickmaking: A Complete Course   *Andrew Jones & Clive George*
Stickmaking Handbook   *Andrew Jones & Clive George*
Storage Projects for the Router   *GMC Publications*
Test Reports: *The Router* and *Furniture & Cabinetmaking*
    GMC Publications

Veneering: A Complete Course — *Ian Hosker*
Veneering Handbook — *Ian Hosker*
Woodfinishing Handbook (Practical Crafts) — *Ian Hosker*
Woodworking with the Router: Professional
Router Techniques any Woodworker can Use
Bill Hylton & Fred Matlack

UPHOLSTERY

The Upholsterer's Pocket Reference Book — *David James*
Upholstery: A Complete Course (Revised Edition) — *David James*
Upholstery Restoration — *David James*
Upholstery Techniques & Projects — *David James*
Upholstery Tips and Hints — *David James*

TOYMAKING

Scrollsaw Toy Projects — *Ivor Carlyle*
Scrollsaw Toys for All Ages — *Ivor Carlyle*

DOLLS' HOUSES AND MINIATURES

1/12 Scale Character Figures for the Dolls' House — *James Carrington*
Americana in 1/12 Scale: 50 Authentic Projects
Joanne Ogreenc & Mary Lou Santovec
Architecture for Dolls' Houses — *Joyce Percival*
The Authentic Georgian Dolls' House — *Brian Long*
A Beginners' Guide to the Dolls' House Hobby — *Jean Nisbett*
Celtic, Medieval and Tudor Wall Hangings in 1/12 Scale Needlepoint
Sandra Whitehead
Creating Decorative Fabrics: Projects in 1/12 Scale — *Janet Storey*
The Dolls' House 1/24 Scale: A Complete Introduction — *Jean Nisbett*
Dolls' House Accessories, Fixtures and Fittings — *Andrea Barham*
Dolls' House Furniture: Easy-to-Make Projects in 1/12 Scale — *Freida Gray*
Dolls' House Makeovers — *Jean Nisbett*
Dolls' House Window Treatments — *Eve Harwood*
Easy to Make Dolls' House Accessories — *Andrea Barham*
Edwardian-Style Hand-Knitted Fashion for 1/12 Scale Dolls
Yvonne Wakefield
How to Make Your Dolls' House Special: Fresh Ideas for Decorating
Beryl Armstrong
Make Your Own Dolls' House Furniture — *Maurice Harper*
Making Dolls' House Furniture — *Patricia King*
Making Georgian Dolls' Houses — *Derek Rowbottom*
Making Miniature Chinese Rugs and Carpets — *Carol Phillipson*
Making Miniature Food and Market Stalls — *Angie Scarr*
Making Miniature Gardens — *Freida Gray*
Making Miniature Oriental Rugs & Carpets — *Meik & Ian McNaughton*
Making Period Dolls' House Accessories — *Andrea Barham*
Making Tudor Dolls' Houses — *Derek Rowbottom*
Making Victorian Dolls' House Furniture — *Patricia King*
Miniature Bobbin Lace — *Roz Snowden*
Miniature Embroidery for the Georgian Dolls' House — *Pamela Warner*
Miniature Embroidery for the Tudor and Stuart Dolls' House
Pamela Warner
Miniature Embroidery for the Victorian Dolls' House — *Pamela Warner*
Miniature Needlepoint Carpets — *Janet Granger*
More Miniature Oriental Rugs & Carpets — *Meik & Ian McNaughton*

Needlepoint 1/12 Scale: Design Collections for the Dolls' House
Felicity Price
New Ideas for Miniature Bobbin Lace — *Roz Snowden*
The Secrets of the Dolls' House Makers — *Jean Nisbett*

CRAFTS

American Patchwork Designs in Needlepoint — *Melanie Tacon*
Beginning Picture Marquetry — *Lawrence Threadgold*
Blackwork: A New Approach — *Brenda Day*
Celtic Cross Stitch Designs — *Carol Phillipson*
Celtic Knotwork Designs — *Sheila Sturrock*
Celtic Knotwork Handbook — *Sheila Sturrock*
Celtic Spirals and Other Designs — *Sheila Sturrock*
Complete Pyrography — *Stephen Poole*
Creative Backstitch — *Helen Hall*
Creative Embroidery Techniques Using Colour Through Gold
Daphne J. Ashby & Jackie Woolsey
The Creative Quilter: Techniques and Projects — *Pauline Brown*
Cross-Stitch Designs from China — *Carol Phillipson*
Decoration on Fabric: A Sourcebook of Ideas — *Pauline Brown*
Decorative Beaded Purses — *Enid Taylor*
Designing and Making Cards — *Glennis Gilruth*
Glass Engraving Pattern Book — *John Everett*
Glass Painting — *Emma Sedman*
Handcrafted Rugs — *Sandra Hardy*
How to Arrange Flowers: A Japanese Approach to English Design
Taeko Marvelly
How to Make First-Class Cards — *Debbie Brown*
An Introduction to Crewel Embroidery — *Mave Glenny*
Making and Using Working Drawings for Realistic Model Animals
Basil F. Fordham
Making Character Bears — *Valerie Tyler*
Making Decorative Screens — *Amanda Howes*
Making Fabergé-Style Eggs — *Denise Hopper*
Making Fairies and Fantastical Creatures — *Julie Sharp*
Making Greetings Cards for Beginners — *Pat Sutherland*
Making Hand-Sewn Boxes: Techniques and Projects — *Jackie Woolsey*
Making Knitwear Fit — *Pat Ashforth & Steve Plummer*
Making Mini Cards, Gift Tags & Invitations — *Glennis Gilruth*
Making Soft-Bodied Dough Characters — *Patricia Hughes*
Natural Ideas for Christmas: Fantastic Decorations to Make
Josie Cameron-Ashcroft & Carol Cox
New Ideas for Crochet: Stylish Projects for the Home — *Darsha Capaldi*
Papercraft Projects for Special Occasions — *Sine Chesterman*
Patchwork for Beginners — *Pauline Brown*
Pyrography Designs — *Norma Gregory*
Pyrography Handbook (Practical Crafts) — *Stephen Poole*
Rose Windows for Quilters — *Angela Besley*
Rubber Stamping with Other Crafts — *Lynne Garner*
Sponge Painting — *Ann Rooney*
Stained Glass: Techniques and Projects — *Mary Shanahan*
Step-by-Step Pyrography Projects for the Solid Point Machine
Norma Gregory
Tassel Making for Beginners — *Enid Taylor*
Tatting Collage — *Lindsay Rogers*
Tatting Patterns — *Lyn Morton*
Temari: A Traditional Japanese Embroidery Technique — *Margaret Ludlow*
Trip Around the World: 25 Patchwork, Quilting and Appliqué Projects
Gail Lawther

GARDENING

PHOTOGRAPHY

ART TECHNIQUES

VIDEOS

MAGAZINES

WOODTURNING ◆ WOODCARVING
FURNITURE & CABINETMAKING
THE ROUTER ◆ NEW WOODWORKING
THE DOLLS' HOUSE MAGAZINE
OUTDOOR PHOTOGRAPHY
BLACK & WHITE PHOTOGRAPHY
MACHINE KNITTING NEWS
BUSINESSMATTERS

The above represents a full list of all titles currently published
or scheduled to be published.
All are available direct from the Publishers or through
bookshops, newsagents and specialist retailers.
To place an order, or to obtain a complete catalogue, contact:

**GMC Publications,
Castle Place, 166 High Street, Lewes,
East Sussex BN7 1XU United Kingdom
Tel: 01273 488005 Fax: 01273 478606
E-mail: pubs@thegmcgroup.com**

Orders by credit card are accepted